. . . who shut up the sea with doors, when it brake forth, as if it had issued out of the womb? When I made the cloud the garment thereof, and thick darkness a swaddling-band for it, and brake up for it my decreed place, and set bars and doors, and said, Hitherto shalt thou come, but no further: and here shall thy proud waves be stayed?

JOB 38:8-11

And I heard a great voice out of heaven saying, Behold, the tabernacle of God is with men, and he will dwell with them, and they shall be his people, and God himself shall be with them, and be their God. And God shall wipe away all tears from their eyes: and there shall be no more death, neither sorrow, nor crying, neither shall there be any more pain: for the former things are passed away. And he that sat upon the throne said, Behold, I make all things new.

REVELATION 21:3-5

The Doors of the Sea

Where Was God in the Tsunami?

David Bentley Hart

William B. Eerdmans Publishing Company

Grand Rapids, Michigan / Cambridge, U.K.

© 2005 Wm. B. Eerdmans Publishing Co.
All rights reserved

Wm. B. Eerdmans Publishing Co.
255 Jefferson Ave. S.E., Grand Rapids, Michigan 49503 /
P.O. Box 163, Cambridge CB3 9PU U.K.

Printed in the United States of America

10 09 08 07 06 05   7 6 5 4 3 2 1

ISBN 0-8028-2976-7

www.eerdmans.com

For Robert Wilken

Contents

Acknowledgments

―――――

This book springs from a brief column that appeared in the "Houses of Worship" section of *The Wall Street Journal* on Friday, December 31, 2004, under the title "Tremors of Doubt." After it appeared, I was asked to write a longer opinion column, expanding the argument, for the March 2005 issue of *First Things;* that column appeared under the title "Tsunami and Theodicy."

I wish to thank Bill Eerdmans for suggesting that I write this book, and for making such an effort to bring it expeditiously to press. He recognized before I did that the reaction elicited by my original column required a somewhat more deliberate and reflective set of responses than would have been possible by means of discrete exchanges of e-mails. I should thank also my various interlocutors in the weeks following the column, all of whom forced me to articulate my views in greater detail (if not

ix

necessarily with conspicuously greater clarity) than I initially had. I cannot name them all, and some might not wish me to name them in any event, as the conversations in which we were involved — at a time when the horror of the catastrophe was still weighing upon many persons' minds — were sometimes characterized more by heat than by light. I must, though, express special gratitude to Anthony Esolen for the eloquence and passion of his many remarks, and for the effort of thought they provoked in me. I thank John Betz for his advice and support, and for his friendship; encouragement from a scholar and philosophical theologian of such gifts must naturally confirm me in my purpose.

This book is dedicated to Robert Wilken, with great esteem, and in gratitude for his supererogatory support for my work over the years, for his innumerable efforts on my behalf, and for having been the first to express approbation for the theological sentiments expressed in the column from which this book sprang. I would not presume to suggest that he will approve of everything I have said here, but I hope he may. To my wife Solwyn, my love and gratitude for her patience. And to my son Patrick, without whose assistance (as P. G. Wodehouse said somewhere of his daughter) this book would have been completed in half the time, all love and all joy.

꧁ *1* ꧂

Universal Harmony

I

In that great verdant arc of lands that forms the north-
eastern rim of the Indian Ocean and that takes the Bay of
Bengal into its embrace — sweeping out from Sri Lanka
and up the coasts of eastern India to Bangladesh and
Burma, then down the Malay Peninsula to Thailand and
Malaysia, and then further down the coast of Sumatra to
the western tip of Java — there are Gods without number.
Hinduism, in the full profusion of its various forms, is of
course the dominant religion only of India, the Tamils of
Sri Lanka, and the greater Indian diaspora of Southeast
Asia. At one time or another, however, the Vedic deities
have held sway over all these shores; among the Hina-
yana Buddhist peoples of the region — the Sinhalese of
Sri Lanka and most of the native inhabitants of Thailand

and Burma (or Myanmar, if one prefers) — they have always enjoyed a high, if subordinate, eminence in the order of religious devotions. The Chinese communities of the Malay Peninsula and Indonesia, being Mahayana Buddhist for the most part, but also Taoist and Confucian, are attended by bodhisattvas and divinities of a more remote provenance. Islam is the official faith of Bangladesh and Malaysia, and the dominant religion of Indonesia. Christianity, Catholic and Protestant, has a presence in all these lands, in some cases small but substantial, in others somewhat more fugitive and beleaguered. As for the aboriginal animisms of the indigenous peoples, such as the *Nat* worship of Burma, none of the great faiths of the far or near East has succeeded in extinguishing them. And — needless to say, perhaps — in very many places the demarcations between differing traditions are lost in a golden haze of generous and unreflective syncretism. Very few of those who live at the upper periphery of the Indian Ocean doubt that, among the many supernal powers keeping watch over those waters — benign or capricious, transcendent or local, omnipotent or merely mighty — there is at least one who is able to govern their tides and turbulences and to keep the sea within its appointed bounds.

Far below the water's surface, however, at and beneath the ocean floor, lies a source of elemental violence so vast, convulsive, unpredictable, perennial, and destructive that one might almost be tempted to think that it is itself a particularly indomitable and infernal sort of god. And, in fact, the most enduring manifestations of its power above sea level — those grim volcanic islands that lie in a long catenate archipelago off the western shores of Indonesia — have in their time no doubt been objects of worship, supplication, propitiation, and pious dread. These islands are situated along perhaps the most volatile geodynamic fissure in the world, the place where apparently two enormous tectonic plates — the Indo-Australian and the Eurasian (upon whose edge Sumatra and Java are precariously poised) — continuously pass one another by in their slow, interminable, millennial migrations. It is an immense seam of unquenchable fire that down through the geological epochs has shaped and reshaped this entire crescent of islands and continental littorals. Its forces do not subside, and it is never truly dormant; but it does know long intervals of comparative stability, during which life above goes on largely undisturbed. Up there, when the weather is calm, the water is a smooth, immeasurable, tremulous mirror of the tropical sky, gleaming like silver, furling with crystalline brilliancy, its waves sapphire blue at their crests and a deep glassy green in their inner folds. Tourists — upon whom many of the countries of the region so desperately depend —

come by the thousands in order (for the most part) to luxuriate on ivory beaches and gaze out at the beauty of the ocean and marvel at the extravagant lushness of the South Asian flora.

On good days, it must be all but impossible to imagine the slow, constant, savage geological ferment so many fathoms down. When, though, the power lurking below the marine fault does break forth with full strength, the devastation it wreaks is more terrible than the mind can easily encompass. It was here, for instance, in 1883, in the Strait of Sunda between Sumatra and Java, that the entire island of Krakatoa exploded, killing more than 36,000 persons. All but a minuscule minority died not from the burning ash flung into the air by the blast, but from the massive tsunamis that followed from it. Tens of thousands of men, women, and children drowned on land, or were carried out to sea, or were shattered by the force of the water. It appears, moreover, that this same volcano had erupted in similar fashion many times in the past, only to form itself anew. Even now, it is growing into an island again in the broad mouth of the Sunda Strait, storing up fire for its next eruption. And, of course, earthquakes are inevitable. As the tectonic plates move, they must on occasion grate against one another, impede one another's drift, then jolt free. When this happens, the heavier basalt of the ocean floor can even actually slide beneath and raise the lighter continental shelf. When this occurs, it may be as if the doors of the sea have been flung wide again. The ocean breaks from its confines with annihilating power, and God — it seems — does not stay its waves.

So it was on the second day of Christmas 2004, when an earthquake — measured on the Richter scale at a magnitude of 9.0 — struck offshore of Banda Aceh, at the northern end of Sumatra, early in the morning. Near the epicenter, the tremors were horribly lethal; but the far greater devastation released by the quake came (as is almost always the case) from the tsunamis it drove toward all the surrounding coasts. An enormous surge, scarcely visible at first, spread in all directions with extraordinary speed, then slowed and mounted as it approached land, and then struck with cataclysmic ferocity. No one was prepared. Warnings may have been given to some of the regional governments, but they were not made public. At the shorelines, the lovely glistening hyaline waters were all at once polluted with the silt and debris and murk of the ocean's bed, and rose with such terrifying suddenness that very few — even as far away as Sri Lanka — had sufficient time to flee.

In the days immediately following, a proper picture of the real dimensions of the disaster was strangely slow in reaching the world beyond. At first, those of us who lived far from the region heard that thousands had perished, which seemed tragic enough; then, in subsequent days, the number of the dead began to be reckoned in tens of thousands; and then, finally, in hundreds of thousands, and the true horror of what had occurred became in some small measure appreciable for us. As I write, the most recent estimate is very near a quarter million. And when images of the aftermath began to appear, they seemed too dreadful to believe: films of those caught amid the flood clinging desperately to poles and railings, and occasionally losing their grip to be torn away by the fierce rush of the water; satellite pictures showing where whole islands had been laid waste, villages swept away, the earth stripped of vegetation; and photographs of long stretches of coastline strewn not only with wreckage but with countless corpses, a great many the corpses of small children.

Considering the scope of the catastrophe, and of the agonies and sorrows it had visited on so many, we should probably have all remained silent for a while. The claim to discern some greater meaning — or, for that matter, meaninglessness — behind the contingencies of history and nature is both cruel and presumptuous at such times. Pious platitudes and words of comfort seem not only futile and banal, but almost blasphemous; meta-physical disputes come perilously close to mocking the dead. There are moments, simply said, when we probably ought not to speak. But, of course, we must speak.

II

It is difficult to tell sometimes, in the wake of a great disaster, whether those who hasten to announce whatever greater significance they find in the event are moved more by an urgent moral need to sow light in the midst of darkness or by a kind of emotional and rhetorical opportunism, which takes the torments of others as an occasion for the reiteration of one or another set of personal convictions. I can scarcely, I hasten to say, be very sanctimonious on this score: I myself agreed to produce a short column on the Indian Ocean catastrophe for *The Wall Street Journal* on the Friday following the earthquake. But it is hard not to suspect (uncharitably, perhaps) an especially glacial and doctrinaire callousness on the part of the triumphalistic atheist who feels compelled to leap at once into the breach and stridently to proclaim that here, finally, the materialist creed has been vindicated: that here we have an instance of empirical horrors too vast to be reconciled with belief in a loving and omnipotent God, and that upon this rock the ship of faith must surely founder and sink and leave nothing but fragments of flotsam to wash up into the shoals of the future.

The vice is especially pronounced among journalists, as might be expected: for, naturally, if one believes that God's last defenses have been dashed aside, and that the *coup de grâce* can now be dealt, one does not wish to be beaten to press. Which is not to say that other, more commendable motives are not also at work: no doubt the fanatical materialist and the captious skeptic often need to give voice to a genuine moral outrage, and this is nothing contemptible. But the alacrity with which some seize upon the moment when tragedy befalls to hold forth upon the indifference of the universe and the obvious nonexistence of God inevitably gives rise, at the very least, to extraordinarily inept arguments; and this in itself suggests a certain want of care or scrupulous reflection. After all, if one considers the implications of an event like the Indian Ocean disaster in a broader perspective than is provided in the first few moments, and asks what it has taught us about the world we live in or the nature of finitude that we did not already know perfectly well, the answer — to be unsentimentally precise — is absolutely nothing.

This is not to ignore the pitiless immensity of what happened that day, nor certainly to dismiss the spiritual perplexity that misery on so awful a scale occasions. But there comes a point when prudence, no less than intellectual honesty, requires us — Christians, that is — to prepare ourselves for what must inevitably follow: the perorations and tirades of secular moralists, gravely and condescendingly informing us that the last slender supports for our irrational religious allegiances have been ripped away, and exhorting us to repent at last of our savage credulity. Christian forbearance can all too easily falter at such junctures and give way to anger if one has not cultivated some degree of equanimity in advance. In the aftermath of the wreck of so many thousands of lives, it would be somewhat wicked to yield to petty annoyances. But, obviously, it is hard not to become impatient at disquisitions on the absurdity of religious beliefs confidently delivered by persons who have made no discernible effort to ascertain what those beliefs actually are. It seems a curious delusion — but apparently it is one shared by a great number of the more passionate secularists — to imagine that Christianity has never at any point during the two millennia of its intellectual tradition considered the problem of evil, or confronted the reality of suffering and death, or at any rate responded to these things with any subtlety: that Christians have down through the centuries simply failed to notice every single instance of flood, earthquake, or tempest, pestilence, famine, or fire, war, genocide, or slaughter; or that every Christian who has been crippled, or has contracted a terminal illness, or has watched his wife die of cancer, or has stood at the graveside of his child has somehow remained inexplicably insensible to the depths of his own pain and to the dark moral and metaphysical enigmas haunting every moment of his grief.

The British journalist Martin Kettle, for instance, published a column in *The Guardian* two days after the catastrophe that, in its logic and in its tone, seemed on first reading (not to put too fine a point on it) excruciatingly fatuous. "Earthquakes and the belief in the judgment of God are . . . very hard to reconcile," he declares. When confronting an event like the Sumatran disaster, he argues, only two explanations as to its cause are possible: either one that is "purely natural" or "some other kind" (as though there must be some conflict between a naturalistic elucidation of contingent causes and the doctrine of creation, or as if God were to be imagined as some finite cause among the world's other causes — a particular worldly agency — who must occupy a place in the sequence of natural events akin to that of a shifting tectonic plate). The scientific explanation is uncomforting but internally coherent; but what, he asks, of the view of "creationists"? How can they possibly look upon destruction so vast and indiscriminate and continue to believe in the workings of a divine intelligence behind the fabric of nature? "What God sanctions an earthquake? What God protects against it? Why does the quake strike these places and these peoples and not others?" Clearly, Kettle is convinced, no very impressive answer to such questions ever has been or ever will be ventured. But Kettle is also uncertain that there are many at present as bold as he in pressing these questions. Confident though he is in the justice of his plaint, he concludes by reflecting upon proposed laws in Britain forbidding expressions of religious hatred, which he fears might restrict open critique of religious beliefs, and morosely wonders whether most of his contemporaries still have the courage to join him in his mission to *écraser l'infâme,* or whether they are now "too cowed" even to ask if indeed "the God can exist that can do such things." (Of course, all things being equal, it is fairly safe to say that a public avowal of atheism will not require any particularly plentiful reserves of courage in Britain in the foreseeable future.)

A somewhat less portentous — but even more combative — article by Ron Rosenbaum appeared in the January 10 edition of *The New York Observer,* which laid out the same conventional assortment of arguments at greater (and rather more tedious) length, but did so in a way that suggested an at least fitful acquaintance with the sort of debates that, in the past few centuries, have been conducted between atheists and (it is necessary to emphasize this term) *theists*. This is not to say that Rosenbaum is acutely clear as to his terms. He defines "theodicy" quite accurately as "the attempt to reconcile the idea of an all-powerful, just and loving God who intervenes in history ... with the recurrence of catastrophic slaughter from 'natural' causes such as tsunamis and man-made evils such as genocides"; but he also calls theodicy a "subdiscipline of theology," which it most definitely is not. Nor, clearly, is he a trained philosopher, as his audacious but reckless attempt to summarize and then criticize Leibniz's theodicy makes obvious. Nor, certainly, does he address what Christian theology has traditionally said over the centuries about the nature of evil, principally because he clearly has no idea what that is. But, presumptuous as it is, Rosenbaum's article does possess many very real virtues: it is contemptuous of facile and evasive theodicies that seek somehow to disencumber God of his omnipotence; it is marked by a salutary scorn for any view of divine sovereignty that amounts to little more than the fatalistic adoration of a celestial despot; it is equally merciless in its derision of those who treat natural calamities as direct acts of divine retribution and of those who find evidences of divine benignity in isolated anecdotes of implausible survival amid the general ruin; and it is written with the awareness that if what happened in the Indian Ocean is a challenge to any kind of religious belief, it is the belief in a God of consummate goodness: a God of love.

It is, of course, extremely tempting simply to dismiss arguments such as Kettle's and Rosenbaum's as irrelevancies (I confess this was my own initial reaction to both). They often seem to take issue, after all, with a God of their own devising. Rosenbaum, for example, mentions a somewhat famous article by J. L. Mackie from 1955 that argues that we must conclude from the evidences of history and nature that if God is indeed omnipotent, he manifestly is not good, and that if he is good, he manifestly is not omnipotent. It is an argument, says Rosenbaum, that so far no one has succeeded in refuting. In point of fact, though, there is no argument here to refute; the entire case is premised upon an inane anthropomorphism — abstracted from any living system of belief — that reduces God to a finite ethical agent, a limited psychological personality, whose purposes are measurable upon the same scale as ours, and whose ultimate ends for his creatures do not transcend the cosmos as we perceive it. This is not to say that it is an argument without considerable emotional and even moral force; but of logical force there is none. Unless one can see the beginning and end of all things, unless one possesses a divine, eternal vantage upon all of time, unless one knows the precise nature of the relation between divine and created freedom, unless indeed one can fathom *infinite* wisdom, one can draw no conclusions from finite experience regarding the coincidence in God of omnipotence and perfect goodness. One may still hate God for worldly suffering, if one chooses, or deny him, but one cannot in this way "disprove" him.

At some level, it is even tempting to think that since strict materialism is among the most incoherent of superstitions — one that has never really asked the question of the being of things in any depth or with any persistence, or one that has at best attempted to conjure that question away as a fallacy of grammar — it is incapable of imagining any conception of God more sophisticated than its own. The materialist encounters an instance of unjust suffering and, by a sort of magical thinking, concludes from the absence of any immediately visible moral order that there must be nothing transcendent of material causality, in much the same way that certain of our more remote, primitive ancestors might have seen a flash of lightning in the sky and concluded that some god must have flung it from on high. In neither case does the conclusion follow from the evidence (though in the latter case the reasoning is somewhat more rigorous); and in neither case is the god at issue much more than an affective myth.

It is, as I say, *tempting* thus to dismiss such arguments,

and then simply to ignore them; but one should not. For, if one grant them a second thought, or a third, one must sooner or later concede that they are not quite as vapid as it would be convenient to think. For one thing, while they may not be particularly germane to Christian theological tradition, they are nonetheless responses to the way in which many religious persons (including many Christians) are in the habit of speaking. More to the point, though, there are even certain respects in which arguments of this sort should command not only the attention of Christians, but some measure of their sympathy — not pity, that is to say, not a patronizing longanimity, but sympathy in the proper sense of kindred feeling. After all, at the heart of all such unbelief lies an undoubtedly authentic moral horror before the sheer extravagance of worldly misery, a kind of rage for justice, a refusal of easy comfort, and an unwillingness to be reconciled to evil that no one who believes this to be a fallen world should want to disparage. For the secret irony pervading these arguments is that they would never have occurred to consciences that had not in some profound way been shaped by the moral universe of a Christian culture.

III

The *locus classicus* of modern disenchantment with "nature's God" is surely Voltaire's *Poëme sur le désastre de Lisbonne,* occasioned by the great earthquake that struck offshore of Lisbon on All Saints' Day, 1755. The city was at that time perhaps the most resplendent capital in Europe, the center of the vast Portuguese Empire, a seat of learning, a garden of the arts, and home to a quarter of a million persons. As it was a feast day, a Sunday, and morning, most of Lisbon was at church when the earthquake came in three successive tremors, estimated now (like the Sumatran earthquake) at a Richter force of 9.0. Crevices opened in the streets as wide as fifteen feet across. Many thousands died in those first moments, crushed beneath falling buildings. Thousands more, who had fled to the mouth of the Tagus River to escape the destruction in the city, were killed in boats or along the riverbanks by the massive tsunami that was cast up on shore more than half an hour after the initial shock. Before long, an enormous fire began to consume the ruined city, as well as those who — like the invalid patients in the Hospital Real — were unable to run from the flames. In all, at least 60,000 perished in the city, and probably very many more. And the tsunami spread death all along the coasts of Portugal's Algarve, Southern Spain, and North Africa; in Morocco,

10,000 were killed. So enormous was the earthquake that it was felt in Sweden and Finland, and so powerful were the waves it sent out from its epicenter that the water could be seen to rise steeply several hours later in the Antilles, Antigua, Martinique, and Barbados.

Voltaire was not an atheist; he was a deist of the most austere variety, whose reverent admiration for the God who had made the universe and then left it to its own immanent devices was evidently quite genuine. His poem was a lacerating attack not on the idea of a creator God, but on the sort of theodicy that had become standard by his time, that odd, bland metaphysical optimism — most scintillatingly expressed in Pope's *Essay on Man*, but derived from the works of Leibniz, Shaftesbury, and Bolingbroke — that says that this is the "best of all possible worlds," and that thus *"tout est bien."* Setting aside the vexatious question of whether Voltaire ever properly understood the complexity of Leibniz's system (mostly because there really is no question about it; he did not), he certainly grasped the imbecility of popular theodicy's attempts to explain away cosmic evil by appeal to "universal laws" that have been set in place to assure the greatest *possible* good for creatures and that are therefore, necessarily, binding even upon God.

While Voltaire was no friend of Christianity, his poem's preface does distinguish between this sort of theodicy and Christian teaching. Moreover, at both the beginning and the end of the preface, he affirms and even in some sense invokes (who can say with how much sincerity) the rule of divine providence. This demonstrates at the very least that he understood the difference between the belief in a providential order in history and the belief that God has simply designed the world as it now is, as a kind of metaphysical machine perpetually preserving a precise cosmic equilibrium between morality and felicity, and between life and death, for the sake of our present well-being.

For the latter view, Voltaire holds none of his contempt in reserve. His poem possesses what one can only call an exquisite savagery, made all the more effective by the fine, smooth, mellifluous polish of his alexandrines. He invites all philosophers who say that "all is well" to come and contemplate the wrack and ruin of Lisbon — its debris, shreds, and cinders — and explain by what calculus of the universal good they can reckon the cosmic necessity of

Ces femmes, ces enfants l'un sur l'autre entassés,
Sous ces marbres rompus ces membres dispersés;
Cent mille infortunés que la terre dévore,
Qui, sanglants, déchirés, et palpitants encore,
Enterrés sous leurs toits, terminent sans secours
Dans l'horreur du tourment leurs lamentable jours!

[These women, these infants heaped one upon the other, these limbs scattered beneath shattered marbles; the hundred thousand unfortunates whom the earth devours, who — bleeding and torn, still palpitating, interred beneath their roofs — end their lamentable days without comfort, amid the horror of their torment!]

Looking upon all of this, Voltaire asks the metaphysical optimist, would you dare state that what you see is nothing more than the effect of eternal laws, which must determine even the will of a God both free and good? Or would you perhaps argue that all of this is merely God's just vengeance upon human iniquity? But then

Quel crime, quelle faute ont commis ces enfants
Sur le sein maternel écrasés et sanglants?

[What crime and what sin have they committed, these infants crushed and bleeding on their mothers' breasts?]

Either response, in the face of such suffering, is manifestly repellent; for those who speak in such terms, sufficient disdain seems scarcely possible — to judge, at least, from one particularly scornful apostrophe:

Tranquilles spectateurs, intrépides esprits,
De vos frères mourants contemplant les naufrages,
Vous recherchez en paix les causes des orages . . .

[Tranquil spectators, intrepid spirits, contemplat-
ing the shipwreck of your dying brothers you search
in peace for the causes of the storm . . .].

Quite apart from its moral hideousness, is this sort of
theodicy even passingly credible?

Tout est bien, dites-vous, et tout est nécessaire.
Quoi! l'univers entier, sans ce gouffre infernal,
Sans engloutir Lisbonne, eût-il été plus mal?

[All is well, you say, and all is necessary. What? The
entire universe, but for this infernal abyss engulfing
Lisbon, would have been worse off?]

Would it indeed bring solace, asks Voltaire, to the "sad
inhabitants of desolate shores, amid the horror of their
torments," to know that others will profit from their de-
mise, and that by their downfall they have discharged
the role prescribed for them by universal and inviolable
law? Does the entire incessant, pitiless, blood-drenched
cycle of life and death become endurable, and even mor-

ally beautiful, because some sort of "general happiness" can be said to arise out of the whole "fatal chaos of individual miseries"? If indeed the theodicist would have us believe that the present order of the world is a "great chain of being" whose intricate calibrations and balances are so delicately and cunningly poised that not even God dare alter any detail of its arrangement, then it is obvious to Voltaire that the theodicist is speaking risible nonsense:

Non, ne présentez plus à mon coeur agité
Ces immuables lois de la nécessité,
Cette chaine des corps, des esprits et des mondes.
O rêves de savants! ô chimères profondes!
Dieu tient en main la chaîne, et n'est point enchaîné;
Par son choix bienfaisant tout est déterminé;
Il est libre, il est juste, il n'est point implacable.
Pourquoi donc souffrons-nous sous
            un maître équitable?

[No, no longer place these immutable laws of necessity before my agitated heart, this chain of bodies, spirits, and worlds. O the dreams of savants! O how profoundly chimerical! God holds the chain in his hand, and he is not in any way enchained; by his beneficent will all is determined; he is free, he is

just, he is never implacable. Why then do we suffer
under so equitable a master?]

And on the poem goes, for a total of 234 lines, one glit-
tering heroic couplet following upon another, until all
Voltaire's indignation is spent. His verse lacks the epi-
grammatic and syntactic brilliance of Pope's, of course;
but, such is its rhetorical and moral force that it leaves a
far deeper impression (or perhaps some might say cau-
terization) upon the mind than anything in the *Essay on
Man*.

As I have already noted, however, Voltaire's poem is
not directly concerned with the God of Christian doctrine. Rather, it concerns a God who directly governs a
cosmos that is exactly as he intended it (or as he had to
intend it), balancing out all its many eventualities and
particularities in a sort of infinite equation that leaves no
remainder — no irredeemable evil, no irrecuperable absurdity — behind. Nowhere does Voltaire address the
Christian belief in an ancient alienation from God that
has wounded creation in its uttermost depths and re-
duced cosmic time to a shadowy vestige of the world God
truly intends, and enslaved creation to spiritual and terrestrial powers hostile to God; nor certainly does he concern himself with the biblical narrative of redemption.
His poem is an artifact of a particular moment in West-

ern intellectual history — post-Christian but not yet post-theist — and as such represents a debate not between atheism and faith but between two opposing schools of deism. Seen thus, it casts a purifying light upon the more maladroit and atheistic polemic of later skeptics.

So much is Voltaire's jeremiad a relic of philosophical controversies that have all but entirely died out, and of pictures of God that have long been effaced from all cultural consciousness, that it reminds us always to ask — when confronting something like Martin Kettle's diatribe or J. L. Mackie's famous but surreally inapposite argument — precisely what God it is we are talking about. Has any living faith ever enjoined anyone to believe in the God in whom Kettle and Mackie are so desperate for us not to believe? (Certainly, I imagine, it would take no great effort on our part to oblige them.) Has anyone ever worshipped this God, or been willing to die — or kill — for him? Certainly none of those countless deities who preside over the waters of the Indian Ocean meet the description. The God of those vanished theodicies, with whom Mackie felt it profitable to continue to grapple, is certainly not the boundlessly glorious and terrifying God revealed to Arjuna in the theophany of the eleventh book of the *Bhagavad Gita,* into whose innumerable blazing mouths men and gods and entire worlds fly to their destruction. He is not any of the lesser deities whom Hindus and Buddhists alike believe to be no less bound by karma than we. Much less is he any of those native spirits of Southeast Asia who dwell within or behind all of living nature's multitudinous forms. He is not even the God of Islam, who orders everything by his illimitable and sovereign will, but who creates the world not for any end immanent to itself, but as an occasion for the creature to submit to his will and to accumulate works of righteousness. So, once more, what God is this?

Again, however, though it is tempting to let the matter rest here, one cannot. As before, in the case of less refined arguments, the more objectively one considers Voltaire's poem, the less easy it becomes to pretend that it poses no challenge whatsoever to Christians. Its proximate target may well be a particularly insipid kind of ethical deism, but that does not mean that the scope of every question it poses is limited only to its immediate object. For, if we are honest in asking what God this is that all our skeptics so despise, we must ultimately conclude that, while he is not the God announced by the Christian gospel, he is nevertheless a kind of faint and distorted echo of that announcement. It is Christianity that not only proclaimed a God of infinite goodness but equated that goodness with infinite love. The atheist who argues from worldly suffering, even crudely, against belief in a

God both benevolent and omnipotent is still someone whose moral expectations of God — and moral disappointments — have been shaped at the deepest level by the language of Christian faith. The actual arguments employed may not demonstrate a keen understanding of the Christian tradition, and they may fail strictly in terms of their logic; but they are not directed merely at a phantom, without any substance whatsoever. Behind the mask of this God in whom no one really believes is — at the very least — a memory of the God whom Christians proclaim, or a shadow of a memory. For this reason, the atheist who cannot believe for moral reasons does honor, in an elliptical way, to the Christian God, and so must not be ignored. He demands of us not the surrender of our beliefs but a meticulous recollection on our parts of what those beliefs are, and a definition of divine love that has at least the moral rigor of principled unbelief. This, it turns out, is no simple thing. For sometimes atheism seems to retain elements of "Christianity" within itself that Christians have all too frequently forgotten.

IV

In truth, in the days following the earthquake and tsunami in the Indian Ocean, more unsavory than the spontaneous but predictable effervescence of village atheist cavils were a number of the statements made by persons claiming to speak from Christian convictions. Some it was easy to disregard as symptomatic of one or another particularly noxious pathology: the sadistic bellowing of a self-described "fundamentalist" preacher in Virginia, attributing the disaster to God's wrath against the heathen and exulting in the spectacle of God's sublime cruelty; the cheerful morbidity of another preacher, airily reminding us that some of the countries affected are notorious for the persecution of Christians; the studied and depraved nonchalance of a conservative Catholic journalist, rejoicing that God had sent the tsunami because of the invaluable lesson it had taught us all; and so on. But there were other, more plausible misstatements of Christian teaching that were harder to ignore, and that were for that very reason more disheartening. As irksome as Martin Kettle's argument was, after all, it was still at the end of the day merely unsophisticated in its logic and pompous in its air of didactic solemnity. More exasperating were the attempts of well-intentioned Christians to rationalize the catastrophe in ways that, however inadvertently, succeeded only in making arguments like Kettle's seem all at once both germane and profound.

Such rationalizations, one should note, are never of a single type. They span the whole spectrum of religious sensibility, and (depending on the quarter of the Christian world from which they emanate) can be cold with stoical austerity, moist with lachrymose piety, palely roseate with a sickly metaphysical optimism, earnest with a pained spiritual tenderness. I learned something of this when I was invited to view a number of Christian Web sites in order to respond to queries and critiques of that *Wall Street Journal* column I mentioned above. Much of what was said on these sites was strikingly eloquent, some of it was appallingly silly, but what was most fascinating about all of the remarks taken together was how incompatible the different theological positions they expressed tended to be one with another.

A Calvinist pastor, positively intoxicated by the grandeur of divine sovereignty, proclaimed that the Indian Ocean disaster — like everything else — was a direct expression of the divine will, acting according to hidden and eternal counsels it would be impious to attempt to penetrate, and producing consequences it would be sinful to presume to judge. He also insisted upon uncompromisingly literal interpretations of verses like Isaiah 45:7 ("I make weal and create woe" — or, even, "create evil") and fearlessly equivocal interpretations of verses like Ezekiel 18:32 ("It is not my pleasure that anyone should die, says the Lord GOD") or 33:11 ("It is not my pleasure that the wicked man should die"). Another Calvinist, this time a junior professor at a small college somewhere in the South, archly explained that, in the "Augustinian-Thomistic-Calvinist tradition" — for the sake of argument, let us grant this chimera a moment's life — and in Reformed thought in particular, God may have no need of suffering and death for himself, but suffering and death nevertheless possess an "epistemic significance" for us, insofar as they reveal divine attributes that "might not otherwise be displayed" (one dreads to imagine what those might be). A Catholic scholar and translator whose work I greatly admire contributed a moving expostulation, invoking the Holy Innocents, glorying in our special privilege (not shared even by the angels) of bearing scars like Christ's, recalling that by God's grace our sufferings are permitted to participate in Christ's and thereby in the profoundest mystery of redemption, and advancing the venerable (but dangerous) homiletic conceit that our salvation from sin will result in a higher beatitude than could ever have evolved from an innocence untouched by death. Another Catholic, who was manifestly devout and intelligent, but who (on this occasion, at least) displayed something of an unfortunate knack for making providence sound like karma, argued that all are guilty through original sin but some more than others, that our sense of justice requires us to believe that "punishments and rewards [are] distributed according to our just desserts," that God is the great "balancer of accounts," and that we must suppose that the sufferings of these innocents will bear "spiritual fruit for themselves and all mankind."

As incongruent as the various positions were one with another, one common element was impossible to overlook: each man, solicitous as he was of God's perfect righteousness, clearly seemed to wish to believe that there is a divine plan in all the seeming randomness of nature's violence that accounts for *every* instance of suffering, privation, and loss in a sort of total sum. This is an understandable impulse. That there is a transcendent providence that will bring God's good ends out of the darkness of history — in spite of every evil — no Christian can fail to affirm. But providence (as even Voltaire seems to have understood) is not simply a "total sum" or "infinite equation" that leaves nothing behind.

I will touch upon this more fully below; here, though, it seems worth noting that there is a point at which an explanation becomes so comprehensive that it ceases to explain anything at all, because it has become a mere tautology. In the case of a pure determinism, this is always so. To assert that every finite contingency is solely and unambiguously the effect of a single will working all things — without any deeper mystery of created freedom — is to assert nothing but that the world is what it is, for any meaningful distinction between the will of God and the simple totality of cosmic eventuality has collapsed. If all that occurs, in the minutest detail and in the entirety of its design, is only the expression of one infinite volition that makes no real room within its transcendent determinations for other, secondary, subsidiary but free agencies (and so for some element of chance and absurdity), then the world is both arbitrary and necessary, both meaningful in every part and meaningless in its totality, an expression of pure power and nothing else. Even if the purpose of such a world is to prepare creatures to know the majesty and justice of its God, that majesty and justice are, in a very real sense, fictions of his will, impressed upon creatures by means both good and evil, merciful and cruel, radiant and monstrous — some are created for eternal bliss and others for eternal torment, and all for the sake of the divine drama of perfect and irresistible might. Such a God, at the end of the day, is nothing but will, and so nothing but an infinite brute event; and the only adoration that such a God can evoke is an almost perfect coincidence of faith and nihilism. Quite apart from what I take to be the scriptural and philosophical incoherence of this concept of God, it provides an excellent moral case for atheism — or, for that matter, Gnosticism (but this too I will address below).

Equally problematic, in some ways, if far more spiritually sane, is the view that all suffering and death should be seen as the precisely apportioned and condign recompense for human sin, balancing all accounts and contributing to a final harmony of all things. It is a pleasing vision of things, in some ways, though quite horrifying in others; it is also a vision so pointlessly complex as to verge upon banality. If it gives us comfort to believe that the death of an infant from disease and the death of a serial murderer late in life from a heart attack, congenital madness and innate genius, the long fortunate life of one of nature's Romans and the brief miserable life of a born pauper are all determined by a precise calculation of what each and every one of us deserves, then it is a comfort sustained by absurdity. If nothing else, one might ask, what of all the particular instances of animal suffering (which no conscience should find it easy to ignore as unimportant)? And, anyway, Christ forbade his disciples, in Luke 13:1-5, to believe that there is a secret due proportion between misfortune and culpability: neither those whose blood Pilate mingled with the sacrifices nor those eighteen upon whom the Tower of Siloam fell met their fates on account of some special degree of iniquity on their parts. And he also made it quite clear, in Matthew 20:1-16, that there is no distinction among the rewards reserved for the righteous corresponding to the diversity of their merits: those who labor all the day and those who labor but an hour receive the same wages.

One may of course assert that original sin makes all of us guilty, and so nothing that happens to us can, strictly speaking, be in excess of what we deserve; but, then, this means that the diversity of our fates cannot be said to correspond to the diversity of our desserts, and that salvation, far from "balancing accounts," is utterly gratuitous. Here also it is probably wise to acknowledge the historical limitation placed upon what one can say on this matter. I, for instance, can write only as a representative of Eastern Orthodoxy, and while most of the larger theological differences that are often said to exist between the Eastern and Western Churches are more illusory than real, on the issue of original sin there is at least one difference upon which most scholars are in agreement. While all Christians must believe that we are born in sin — subject to death, corrupted in body and soul, suffering derangements of will and desire, our minds darkened, unable to save ourselves — it is only in Western tradition that the additional idea of an inherited guilt became a conspicuous feature of the concept of original sin, and it is an idea that Orthodoxy has on many occasions explicitly rejected (which is not to say that it is Orthodox teaching that any of us — slaves as we are to the rule of death in all our members — can ever fail to become guilty of transgression when we attain any level of rational autonomy). As to why there should be this difference, various answers have been offered: a notoriously misleading Latin translation of Romans 5:12, for instance, or a more general "mistranslation" of various of the New Testament's central terms, or even the influence of the Roman jurisprudential genius upon the evolution of Latin theology; some argue that, whereas the Eastern tendency has typically been to read certain New Testament metaphors for sin and salvation almost strictly in terms of civil law concerning slavery — the "debt" of the bondsman who is enslaved in the house of death, but who is "redeemed" from slavery by the "ransom" required for manumission — the Western tendency has been to read those same metaphors in terms of criminal law as well, with its concern for forensic culpability and retribution.

While this disparity in emphasis makes little difference, of course, for how the two traditions understand the disposition of "mature souls," it can lead to quite radically divergent conclusions regarding infants. It was as natural, for instance, for Gregory of Nyssa to conclude that infants who died without baptism were all saved (their deaths being their baptism, as it were, since Hades has been overthrown) or for Theodoret of Cyrus to deny that the baptism of infants served for the remission of sins as it was for Augustine, Prosper of Aquitaine, and Fulgentius Ruspensis to believe that unbaptized infants were destined for eternal perdition. (None of these views, as it happens, is established doctrine in either Church.) Needless to say, I believe the Orthodox view to be the more scriptural (which spares me the effort of professing a belief I find repugnant). But there is no need for a retreat to confessional redoubts on this issue. If, by the time of Thomas Aquinas, the eternal destiny of unbaptized infants had come to be understood not as everlasting torment but as a state of perfect natural beatitude, this is obviously because Roman Catholic thought did not *simply* equate inherited guilt with personal fault. In neither tradition, at any rate, is it possible intelligibly to assert that the death of a small child is in some unambiguous sense an expression of divine justice. Christ, after all, assured us that "little children" are the natural citizens of the Kingdom of God (Matt. 19:14; Mark 10:14; Luke 18:16), and so surely it must be the case that at the deepest level the suffering of children is contrary to the law of the Kingdom, and to the pleasure of its King.

In any event, insofar as I could follow the intent of my interlocutors, I felt varying degrees of sympathy for their positions (though, of course, the Catholic views were somewhat more agreeable to an Orthodox palate than were certain of the others). What struck me most forcibly, however, was that in their apparent need to produce an apologia for God that precluded the possibility of any absurd or pointless remainder in the order of creation and redemption, most of them had seemed to allow certain vital aspects of the language of the New Testament to become all but entirely invisible. Little was said about the sheer exorbitance of grace, the "free gift" of salvation (as Paul calls it in Romans 5), that "unjust" mercy that distributes the same rewards to all who have labored, no matter the length of their service, or God's gracious and magnanimous indifference to our "just desserts." And almost nothing was said regarding — and this can scarcely be emphasized enough — the triumphalism of the gospel or the Johannine and Pauline imagery of spiritual and cosmic warfare; no obvious notice was taken of the strange absence of any metaphysical optimism in the New Testament, or of the refusal of any final reconciliation with death — indeed, the mockery of its power. Yes, certainly, there is nothing, not even suffering or death, that cannot be providentially turned toward God's good ends. But the New Testament also teaches us that, in another and ultimate sense, suffering and death — considered in themselves — have no true meaning or purpose at all; and this is in a very real sense the most liberating and joyous wisdom that the gospel imparts.

V

Above I spoke of the moral power of Voltaire's *Poëme*, but of course such judgments are necessarily relative. Voltaire was a man of the eighteenth century and prey to the superstitions of the Enlightenment; thus there was a depth of reflection upon the darker mysteries of existence, and upon the power of the irrational, that was forever closed to him. His mind never passed through the ordeals of nineteenth-century idealism and materialism, the death and rebirth of metaphysics in the years between Kant and Hegel, revolution and Romanticism, Darwinism, or the first real stirrings of an unabashedly explicit nihilism in the wake of Christianity's slow withdrawal from European culture; and, frankly, his personal theology was far too insipid to inspire either angelic or demonic passions, or to arouse any very searching meditations on evil, cosmic or spiritual. His poem is, therefore, a feeble thing indeed compared to the subtler, more unrelenting, more tortured, and more haunting case for "rebellion" against "the will of God" in human suffering that Dostoyevsky placed in the mouth of Ivan Karamazov.

One might think this ironic, perhaps, given the ardor of Dostoyevsky's faith; but, really, it is probably the case that no one who is not a Christian could ever understand the spiritual and moral motives of such a rebellion with anything like sufficient fullness. Certainly it is the case that the Christian Dostoyevsky's treatment of innocent suffering possesses a profundity of which the deist Voltaire was never even remotely capable. Admittedly, Ivan does not much concern himself with the randomness of natural calamity, as Voltaire does; the evils Ivan recounts to his brother Alexey (or Alyosha) are acts not of impersonal nature but of men, for which one can at least assign a clear culpability. But humanity is no less a part of the natural order than earthquakes and floods, and the human propensity for malice should be no less a scandal to the conscience of the metaphysical optimist than the most violent convulsions of the physical world. Whatever else human evil is, it is — considered apart from any religious doctrine — a cosmic constant, ceaselessly pouring forth from hidden springs of brute impulse and aimless will, driven by some deep prompting of nature as we know it, and so it raises all the same questions concerning the world and its maker that are raised by natural disasters: *Unde hoc malum* — Whence this evil? And what sort of God permits it?

Ivan does not really represent himself as an atheist. He refuses to take a firm position on whether God is the creator of man or man the creator of God, in part because the very idea of God is so implausibly wise and holy an achievement for a vicious animal intellect like ours that he is loath to treat it as a trifle or mere fantasy. That said, he insists that God (if God there be) has supplied humanity with finite, "Euclidean" minds, bound to the conditions of time and space, unable to grasp those transcendent designs by which God undoubtedly guides all things toward their final harmony with him and with one another. It is better not to worry, then, about ultimate things; our minds are conformed to the circumstances of this world, which are all that we can meaningfully judge. So, he says, he accepts that there is a God and even that there is an eternal plan that will, in its consummation, bring about a condition of perfect peace and beatitude for all creation; but it is creation, in fact, that Ivan rejects.

This is the splendid perversity and genius of Ivan's (or Dostoyevsky's) argument, which makes it indeed the argument of a rebel rather than of a mere unbeliever. He willingly grants, he says, that all wounds will at the last be healed, all scars will disappear, all discord will vanish like a mirage or like the miserable invention of finite Euclidean minds, and that such will be the splendor of the finale of all things, when that universal harmony is established, that every heart will be satisfied, all anger soothed, the debt for every crime discharged, and everyone made capable of forgiving every offense and even of finding a justification for everything that has ever happened to mankind; and still he rejects the world that God has made, and that final harmony with it. Ivan admits that he is not a sentimentalist, that indeed he finds it difficult to love his neighbor, but the terms of the final happiness God intends for his creatures are greater than his conscience can bear.

To elucidate his complaint, he provides Alyosha with a grim, unremitting, remorseless recitation of stories about the torture and murder of (principally) children — true stories, as it happens, that Dostoyevsky had collected from the press and from other sources. He tells of Turks in Bulgaria tearing babies from their mothers' wombs with daggers, or flinging infants into the air to catch them on bayonets before their mothers' eyes, or playing with babies held in their mothers' arms — making them laugh, enticing them with the bright metal barrels of pistols — only then to fire the pistols into the babies' faces. He tells a story of two parents regularly savagely flogging their seven-year-old daughter, only to be acquitted in court of any wrongdoing. He tells the story of a "cultured and respectable" couple who tortured their five-year-old daughter with constant beatings, and who — to punish her, allegedly, for fouling her bed — filled her mouth with excrement and locked her on freezing nights in an outhouse. And he invites Alyosha to imagine that child, in the bitter chill and darkness and stench of that place, striking her breast with her tiny fist, weeping her supplications to "gentle Jesus," begging God to release her from her misery, and then to say whether anything — the knowledge of good and evil, for instance — could possibly be worth the bleak brutal absurdity of that little girl's torments. He relates the tale of an eight-year-old serf child who, in the days before emancipation, was bound to the land of a retired general and who accidentally injured the leg of his master's favorite hound by tossing a stone. As punishment, the child was locked in a guardroom through the night and in the morning brought out before his mother and all the other serfs, stripped naked, and forced to run before the entire pack of his master's hounds, which were promptly set upon him to tear him to pieces.

What can a finite Euclidean mind make of such things? How, with anything like moral integrity, can it defer its outrage to some promised future where some other justice will be worked, in some radically different reality than the present? Ivan says that he wants to see that final harmony, and to hear the explanation for why such horrors were necessary, but not so as to assent to either. For, while he can go some distance in granting the principle of human solidarity — in sin and retribution — he cannot figure the suffering of children into that final equation without remainder.

What makes Ivan's argument so novel and disturbing

is not that he simply accuses God of failing to save the innocent; in fact, he grants that in some sense God still will "save" them, in part by rescuing their suffering from sheer "absurdity" and showing what part it had in accomplishing the final beatitude of all creatures. Rather, Ivan rejects salvation itself, insofar as he understands it, and on moral grounds. He rejects anything that would involve such a rescue — anything that would make the suffering of children meaningful or necessary. He grants that one day that eternal harmony will be established, and we will discover how it necessitated the torments endured by children. Perhaps mothers will forgive the murderers of their children, and the serf child, his mother, and their master will be reconciled, and all will praise God's justice, and all evils will be accounted for. Or perhaps the damnation of the wicked will somehow balance the score (though how then there can be that final harmony, when the suffering of the victims has already happened and the suffering of their persecutors will persist eternally, Ivan cannot guess). But still, Ivan wants neither harmony nor the knowledge of ultimate truth at such a cost: "for love of man I reject it"; even ultimate truth "is not worth the tears of that one tortured child." Nor, indeed, does he want forgiveness: the mother of that murdered child must not forgive her child's murderer, even if the child himself can forgive. And so, not denying that there is a

God or a divine design in all things, he simply chooses (respectfully) to return his ticket of entrance to God's Kingdom. After all, Ivan asks, if you could bring about a universal and final beatitude for all beings by torturing one small creature to death, would you think the price acceptable?

I am convinced that Ivan's discourse — which he continues, as hardly needs to be said, by reciting his "poem" about "The Grand Inquisitor" — constitutes the only challenge to a confidence in divine goodness that should give Christians serious cause for deep and difficult reflection. Those Christian readers who have found it easy to ignore or dispense with the case that Dostoyevsky constructs for Ivan have not, I submit, fully comprehended that case (or, alternatively, have comprehended it, but adhere to so degenerate a version of Christian doctrine that they can no longer be said to understand the God revealed in Christ). The reason for this (which it is so vital that one should understand) is that, at base, Ivan's is a profoundly and almost prophetically Christian argument. In part this is true because, even in the way Ivan frames his arraignment of the divine purpose in history, there are already foreshadowings of a deeper Christian riposte to the argument. Ivan's ability to imagine a genuinely moral revolt against God's creative and redemptive order has a kind of nocturnal grandeur about it, a Promethean or Romantic or Gnostic audacity that dares to imagine some spark dwelling in the human soul that is higher and purer than the God who governs this world; and, in that very way, his argument carries within itself an echo of the gospel's vertiginous annunciation of our freedom from the "elements" of the world and from the power of the law. Indeed, the tale of the Grand Inquisitor is in some ways a curious hymn of adoration to Christ as the one who is himself the truest "rebel," entering human history with a divine disregard for its internal economies, disrupting it in fact at the deepest level by sowing freedom with almost profligate abandon among creatures who — with very few exceptions — are incapable of receiving it.

But these are only adumbrations and presentiments of a proper response to Ivan's manifesto. A fuller answer is woven throughout the hundreds of pages of the novel that follow. Some critics doubt that any satisfactory answer is given at all (though I think them mistaken); but even those who believe that an answer is given have on many occasions still failed to appreciate (it seems to me) how radical that answer is, principally because they have not appreciated how radical the question is either. Whatever the case, for the Christian, Ivan's argument — taken simply in itself — provides a kind of spiritual hygiene: it is a solvent of the semi-Hegelian theology of the liberal Protestantism of the late nineteenth century, which succeeded in confusing eschatological hope with progressive social and scientific optimism, and a solvent as well as of the obdurate fatalism of the theistic determinist, and of the confidence of rational theodicy, and — in general — of the habitual and unthinking retreat of most Christians to a kind of indeterminate deism. And this, again, marks it as a Christian argument, even if Christian *sub contrario,* because in disabusing believers of facile certitude in the justness of all things, it forces them back toward the more complicated, "subversive," and magnificent theology of the gospel. Ivan's rage against explanation arises from a Christian conscience, and so — even if Ivan cannot acknowledge it — its inner mystery is an empty tomb, which has shattered the heart of nature and history alike (as we understand them) and fashioned them anew.

This is why Ivan's indignation and anguish have a profundity that Voltaire's cannot. Voltaire's poem, again, is no great challenge to Christian faith, because it inveighs against the ethical deist's God of cosmic balance (and where have his temples been erected?). But Ivan's rebellion is something altogether different. Voltaire sees only the terrible truth that the history of suffering and death is not morally intelligible. Dostoyevsky sees — and this bespeaks both his moral genius and his irreducibly Christian view of reality — that it would be far more terrible if it were.

↦ 2 ↤

Divine Victory

I

What — to pose a question so large, indeterminate, and abstract as to border on the meaningless — is "nature" or the "natural world"? Insofar as such terms possess any affective force for us today, they tend to inspire a vague, disingenuous, and rather promiscuous piety. For us, "nature" constitutes a kind of nomadic value, one both incontestable and infinitely plastic, possessing the power not so much to command as to suggest. To live or behave according to nature is for some of us the very definition of sagacity, sanity, or even virtue, though more often than not the "natural" life amounts to little more than a preference for certain categories of consumer products and the pecuniary resources necessary to purchase those products with some regularity. But, as children of the modern scientific age, well indoctrinated in all its reigning metaphysical fideisms, we do not really think that nature is a source of compelling moral truths; it is, we believe, essentially neutral and (since the forces that drive and shape it are nothing but an assortment of purely material dynamisms) mindless. Except for that small number among us who quaintly and unsuccessfully try to live as pagans (or what they imagine pagans to have been), we do not adore the natural world, or make timorous, imploring approaches to whatever numinous powers we think might hide behind its visible aspect; we do not think the realms of vegetal and animal life to be the haunts of invisible, ancient, and perhaps contending intelligences, whom we must appease with magic rites or hold at bay with apotropaic charms; when we pass through the woods or along the edge of a waste, we do not walk in terror of delitescent fiends or sense the eyes of mischievous faeries upon us or feel a fond awe for the *genius loci* through whose precincts we are passing; the vine is not a god to us, nor the stream a daughter of the "lord of sea." The world, in short, is not alive for us in that way; it cannot speak to us or hear us; it is a "disenchanted" world, from which all deities and spirits have been chased away. Its life is a purposeless striving, a succession of necessary consequences following from accidental causes.

And now that we exercise so comprehensive a medical and technological mastery over whole regions of nature at whose mercy our ancestors lived out their lives, we enjoy the unprecedented luxury of being able to render the "natural" at once remote and benign. It is we who summon it, rather than the reverse, and we do so at our pleasure; it dwells with us, not we with it. We are free to sentimentalize or romanticize it, or even weave a veil of empty and unthreatening sanctity around it — until the moment when disease, age, infirmity, or random violence suddenly defeats us, or fire, flood, tempest, volcanic eruption, or earthquake surprises us by vaulting past our defenses. Then nature astonishes and horrifies us with its power, immensity, and sublime indifference. Even at such times, though, it is unlikely that we truly hate it; ours is a disenchanted world because it is one from which our love, reverence, dread, and hatred have all been irrevocably alienated. Nature for us is a single, internally consistent thing, an event, lovely and enticing, then terrible and pitiless, abundant and destructive at once, but moved neither by will nor by intelligence; it is sheer fact.

It has long been fashionable to attribute the disenchantment or "desacralization" of the world to the rise of Christianity, and this is in some sense arguably correct. Under the reign of the one transcendent God, the power of the old gods faded away, the oracles were silenced, the temples despoiled. By turning human eyes and hearts toward the one God in whom all things live, move, and have their being, Christianity freed the human imagination from its subjugation to the cosmic and elemental "principalities," and revealed the world — and all its immanent forces — to be the work of one creative and redemptive will. That said, it is not the case that the Christianity of late antiquity or even of the early and high Middle Ages evacuated the world of supernatural or preternatural agency, or even that it regarded the gods of old merely as myths; it would be truer to say that the church subverted the ancient cosmology by subduing the ancient powers and demoting them to their proper place in the order of a redeemed creation. *Omnia corporalia regentur per Angelos,* wrote Thomas Aquinas — "All corporeal things are governed by the angels" — and he was doing no more than repeating the wisdom of centuries of Christian tradition, especially as enunciated by Dionysius the Areopagite.

Catholic Christianity — East and West — did not abandon antiquity's vision of a world alive in every part, charged with vital intellect; it saw the motive force at the heart of creation not as an unreasoning engine of material causality, but as an ecstasy of spiritual intelligence and desire. The entire cosmos, it was possible to believe, was drawn ever onward by the yearning of all things for the goodness of God. It was possible to believe, indeed, that the principle of all physical and spiritual motion was, in Dante's phrase, "the love that moves the sun and other stars." What had never yet arisen in imagination was "nature" in the modern sense: a closed causal continuum, conceived (by theists) as the intricate artifice of a God whose transcendence is a kind of absence, or (by atheists) as a purely fortuitous event concerning which the absence of any God is the only "transcendent" truth. This is why it was the modern period that gave birth to a distinct species of "natural theology," one that almost exclusively concerned evidences of a designing intelligence, the signs of a craftsman God to be found in the exquisite complexity of his handiwork.

The problem, of course, with constructing a theology around the bare causal relation between a cosmic machine and its divine artisan is that any analogy between the two becomes extremely perilous for the theologian. What sort of craftsman, after all, do the internal mechanisms of nature declare? The natural world overwhelms us with its splendor, its beauty, its immensities and fragilities, its incalculable diversity, its endless combinations of the colossal and the delicate, sweetness and glory, minute intricacies and immeasurable grandeurs. It is easy, and among the most spontaneous movements of the soul, to revere the God glimpsed in the iridescence of flowered meadows, the emerald light of the deep forest, the soft, immaculate blue of distant mountains, the shining volubility of the sunlit sea, the pale, cold glitter of the stars. This is a perfectly wise and even holy impulse.

But, at the same time, all the splendid loveliness of the natural world is everywhere attended — and, indeed, preserved — by death. All life feeds on life, each creature must yield its place in time to another, and at the heart of nature is a perpetual struggle to survive and increase at the expense of other beings. It is as if the entire cosmos were somehow predatory, a single great organism nourishing itself upon the death of everything to which it gives birth, creating and devouring all things with a terrible and impassive majesty. Nature squanders us with such magnificent prodigality that it is hard not to think that something enduringly hideous and abysmal must abide in the depths of life. Considered "from below," from within the system of nature, the force that drives and animates and shapes the whole of the organic world seems to achieve an almost perfectly transparent epitome of itself in those lavishly floriferous but parasitic vines that — urged always upward by a blind, thrusting, idiotic heliotropism — climb toward the light of the sun by choking the life from the trees around which they grow, constantly struggling out of the shadows in their thirst for the light, extending one tenuous tendril after another toward the sun to swell and slowly suffocate the boughs they entwine, until they burgeon forth at the last in such gorgeous and copious flowers that one might forget what had to perish to make such a triumph of beauty possible.

However one chooses to interpret it, the cosmos as we know it is obviously a closed economy of life and death. This is true even on a geological scale. At one point in the *Poëme sur le désastre de Lisbonne,* Voltaire asks the purveyors of theodicy, rather incredulously,

> Étes-vous assurés que la cause éternelle
> Qui fait tout, qui sait tout, qui créa tout pour elle,
> Ne pouvait nous jeter dans ces tristes climats
> Sans former des volcans allumés sous nos pas!

> [Are you sure that the eternal cause that makes all things, knows all things, and creates all things for itself could not have hurled us into these sorry climes without forming kindling volcanoes beneath our feet!]

And yet, as it turns out, if one grants the deist his watchmaker God, the answer seems inevitable. Of course volcanoes are necessary; but for them, and the tectonic instabilities needed to create them, and the seismic shocks that follow from these instabilities, and the oceans of fire that form the earth's mantle, the planet almost certainly could not produce and sustain the atmosphere that incubates and shelters terrestrial life, nor would its soils be so fertile, nor its range of temperatures so equable. Indeed, ironically enough, the extraordinary fecundity and beauty of the northeastern rim of the Indian Ocean is in large part a result of countless millennia of volcanic activity and tectonic strife.

So, then, what sort of God should a *purely* "natural" theology invite us to see? Perhaps a God whose beneficent purposes can indeed be realized only within the rigid constraints of certain logical possibilities to which his power and will are subject — the God, that is, of rational theodicy. But perhaps a God of the purest sublimity instead, creator and destroyer at once, as in Arjuna's vision of Vishnu on the Kuru plain. Or even perhaps some power not so much sublime as monstrous. "All visible objects, man, are but as pasteboard masks," says Captain Ahab, "but in each event . . . some unknown but still reasoning thing puts forth the mouldings of its features from behind the unreasoning mask": "outrageous strength" joined to "inscrutable malice." To put the matter starkly, nature is a cycle of sacrifice, and religion has often been no more than an attempt to reconcile us to this reality. As rational beings, we are conscious of a certain spiritual dignity or freedom or abnormality in our nature that has estranged us from this unbroken cosmic circle, that has made us historical beings, that has burdened us with an awareness of past and future, and so with apprehension and grief; often sacrificial ceremonies and myths merely soothe the anguish of that estrangement by seeming to unite us again to the perennial order of all things. And this sacrificial sense of reality leads quite reasonably, even when religious thought achieves prodigies of metaphysical sophistication, to an image of God *as* sacrifice, as life and death at once, peace and violence, the creative source and consuming end of all things. That glorious theophany in the *Bhagavad Gita,* perhaps the supreme expression of the religious genius of Hinduism, is as perfect and devout a vision of God as the Absolute as any faith has ever produced (not that this is all the *Gita* has to say about God). And when — not in the *Gita,* but at another point in the *Mahabharata* — Karna (the most movingly tragic of the epic's characters) surveys the Kuru plain where the war between the Pandavas and Kauravas will ultimately claim six million lives (his among them) and remarks that it is simply a great table of sacrifice, his observation is a bitter one, but he is saying nothing impious. It may be that to see the face of God in war and in the deaths of millions — no less than in the beauty and variety of living things — is simply spiritual wisdom, and a recognition of the sacred within nature and history alike.

The Christian vision of God and the world, however, and of how God is reflected within his creation, is of a different order. For, while the Christian is enjoined to see the glory of God in all that is, it is not a glory conformed to the dimensions or logic of "nature" as we understand it; in fact, it renders the very category of "nature" mysterious, alters it, elevates it — judges and redeems it. It is this difference that makes a certain distinctly *moral* skepticism regarding Christian beliefs, of the sort described above, conceivable. Indeed, when this particular strain of skepticism is taken to its greatest possible depth, as it can be only by a mind as intensely Christian as Dostoyevsky's, one discovers it to be a shadow cast by the light of the gospel, an echo of the spiritual and moral liberty that Christianity proclaims, and even a kind of unwilling confession of "belief" (though not of course faith), inasmuch as it knows of no God other than the Christian God of infinite mercy who merits the effort of active unbelief.

II

"God is love," says 1 John 4:16, "and he that dwelleth in love dwelleth in God, and God in him." Christian metaphysical tradition, in both the Orthodox East and the Catholic West, asserts that God is not only good but goodness itself, not only true or beautiful but infinite truth and beauty: that all the transcendental perfections are one in

him who is the source and end of all things, the infinite
wellspring of all being. Thus everything that comes from
God must be good and true and beautiful. As he is the
sole source of being — as he is being itself in its transcendent plenitude, beyond all finite being — everything that
is, insofar as it is, is entirely worthy of love. And it is this
love and goodness of God that the Christian is bidden to
find in the entirety of the created order. Writes St.
Bonaventure:

> Qui igitur tantis rerum creaturum splendoribus
> non illustratur caecus est; qui tantis clamoribus
> non evigilat surdus est; qui ex omnibus his
> effectibus Deum non laudat mutis est; qui ex tantis
> indiciis primum principium non advertit stultus
> est. — Aperi igitur oculos, aures spirituales
> admove, labia tua solve et cor tuum appone, ut in
> omnibus creaturis Deum tuum videas, audias,
> laudes, diligas et colas, magnifices et honores, ne
> forte totus contra te orbis terrarum consurgat.

> [Whoever therefore is not illuminated by splendors
> as great as those to be found in created things is
> blind; whoever fails to heed outcries so great is
> deaf; whoever fails to praise God on account of all
> these his effects is mute; whoever does not turn

from such great signs to their first principle is a
fool. — Therefore, open your eyes, rouse the ears of
your spirit, release you lips, and apply your heart,
that you may see, hear, praise, love and worship,
magnify and honor your God in all creatures, or
else perhaps the whole world may rise up against
you.]

And Thomas Traherne, whom one could quote endlessly
and ecstatically on this matter, writes:

> When you enter into [the world], it is an illimited
> field of variety and beauty: where you may lose
> yourself in the multitude of wonders and delights.
> But it is an happy loss to lose oneself in admiration
> at one's own felicity; and to find GOD in exchange
> for oneself. Which we then do when we see Him in
> His gifts, and adore His glory.

And:

> You never enjoy the world aright, till you see how a
> sand exhibiteth the wisdom and power of God; and
> prize in everything the service which they do you,
> by manifesting His glory and goodness to your
> soul. . . . Wine . . . quencheth my thirst . . . but to see

it flowing from His love who gave it unto man,
quencheth the thirst even of the holy angels. . . .
Your enjoyment of the world is never right, till every morning you awake in Heaven: see yourself in
your Father's palace; and look upon the skies and
the earth and the air, as celestial joys. . . . You never
enjoy the world aright, till the sea floweth in your
veins. . . . Till your spirit filleth the whole world, and
the stars are your jewels . . . till you love men so as
to desire their happiness, with a thirst equal to the
zeal of your own; till you delight in God for being
good to all: you never enjoy the world. . . . The world
is a mirror of infinite beauty, yet no man sees it. It is
a temple of majesty, yet no man regards it. It is a region of light and peace, did not men disquiet it. It is
the Paradise of God.

This is not, one can scarcely stress enough, the dic-
tion of the metaphysical optimist. Theodicy knows no
such elations as these. A sound "natural theology" is by
definition sober and (ideally) mildly depressing: since it
cannot assert anything more about the world than that it
possesses a marvelous complexity of design, nor anything more about God than that he is an immeasurably
wise and powerful engineer, it has far more room in its
arguments for the economy of life and death (in all its

brutality) than it has for "paradise." In fact, the principal task of theodicy is to explain why paradise is not a logical possibility. The Christian vision of the world, however, is not some rational deduction from empirical experience, but is a moral and spiritual aptitude — or, rather, a moral and spiritual labor. The Christian eye sees (or should see) a deeper truth in the world than mere "nature," and it is a truth that gives rise not to optimism but to joy.

In *The Brothers Karamazov,* the Staretz (or Elder) Zosima — whom Dostoyevsky modeled upon a real Staretz of the Optina Monastery named Amvrosy, as well as upon various Eastern Christian saints — constitutes a kind of "answer" to Ivan, though not certainly a direct answer. Rather, in his person and in his teachings, he represents so radically different a perspective upon the whole of created reality that it is almost as if he and Ivan inhabit altogether different worlds (and, in a sense, they do). He is most definitely one who sees paradise all around him, now, in the present moment, and who believes that this paradise is real and accessible to anyone who will look for it. But that, of course, begs the question: How can one look for paradise in such a world as this? So Zosima tells Alyosha that one must love not only all of humanity, but all of God's creation: one must love it as a whole and in its every atom; one must love every leaf, every ray of light, every animal, every plant, and even every inanimate thing, until one takes in the whole world with an all-embracing love; one must treat all beasts with measureless tenderness, and should even (though it may seem absurd) ask forgiveness of the birds; above all one must pour out one's heart in the love of children; and, in this ecstasy of universal charity, one will come to see the true mystery of God dwelling in all things, and will come to understand that mystery ever more deeply as each day passes. It is not difficult to recognize in the background of Zosima's discourse the influence of the teachings of St. Isaac the Syrian, so beloved in the Eastern contemplative tradition, and to hear an echo of the most celebrated single passage from Isaac's mystical treatises:

> What is a merciful heart? A heart aflame for all of creation, for men, birds, beasts, demons, and every created thing; the very thought or sight of them causes the merciful man's eyes to overflow with tears. The heart of such a man is humbled by the powerful and fervent mercy that has captured it and by the immense compassion it feels, and it cannot endure to see or hear of any suffering or any grief anywhere within creation. Hence he constantly lifts up tearful prayers for God's care for and mercy upon even unreasoning brutes and enemies of truth and all who do him injury. He prays even

thus for the family of reptiles, on account of that immeasurable, God-like compassion blazing in his heart.

To see the world as it should be seen, and so to see the true glory of God reflected in it, requires the cultivation of charity, of an eye rendered limpid by love. Maximus the Confessor taught that it is only when one has learned to look upon the world with selfless charity that one sees the true inner essence — the logos — of any created thing, and sees how that thing shines with the light of the one divine Logos that gives it being. But what the Christian should see, then, is not simply one reality: neither the elaborate, benign, elegantly calibrated machine of the deists, smoothly and efficiently accomplishing whatever goods a beneficent God and the intractable potentialities of finitude can produce between them; nor a sacred or divine commerce between life and death; nor certainly "nature" in the modern, mechanistic acceptation of that word. Rather, the Christian should see two realities at once, one world (as it were) within another: one the world as we all know it, in all its beauty and terror, grandeur and dreariness, delight and anguish; and the other the world in its first and ultimate truth, not simply "nature" but "creation," an endless sea of glory, radiant with the beauty of God in every part, innocent of all violence. To see in this way is to rejoice and mourn at once, to regard the world as a mirror of infinite beauty, but as glimpsed through the veil of death; it is to see creation in chains, but beautiful as in the beginning of days.

Christians sometimes find it exceedingly difficult to adopt the cosmological idiom of the New Testament, and while this is understandable in many respects, it can also yield extremely unfortunate results. It is strange enough that the skeptic demands of Christians that they account for evil — physical and moral — in a way that draws a perfectly immediate connection between the will of God for his creatures and the conditions of earthly life; it is stranger still when Christians attempt to oblige. For the scriptural understanding of evil has always been more radical and "fantastic" than anything that can be fitted either within a deistic theodicy or, for that matter, within any philosophical indictment of such a theodicy. Christian thought, from the outset, denies that (in themselves) suffering, death, and evil have any ultimate value or spiritual meaning at all. It claims that they are cosmic contingencies, ontological shadows, intrinsically devoid of substance or purpose, however much God may — under the conditions of a fallen order — make them the occasions for accomplishing his good ends.

Perhaps no doctrine strikes non-Christians as more insufferably fabulous than the claim that we exist in the long melancholy aftermath of a primordial catastrophe: that this is a broken and wounded world, that cosmic time is a phantom of true time, that we live in an umbratile interval between creation in its fullness and the nothingness from which it was called, that the universe languishes in bondage to the "powers" and "principalities" of this age, which never cease in their enmity toward the Kingdom of God. Such language, of course, can strike even many Christians as mythological and dualistic. Some, certainly, seem to fear that if they lend too much credence to the idea of a fallen order actively opposed to God, they will thereby commit themselves to a form of fundamentalist literalism. Alternatively, there are those who suffer from a palpably acute anxiety regarding the honor due the divine sovereignty. Certainly many Christians over the centuries have hastened to resituate the New Testament imagery of spiritual warfare securely within the one all-determining will of God, fearing that to deny that evil and death are the "left hand" of God's goodness in creation or the necessary "shadow" of his righteousness would be to deny divine omnipotence as well.

Nevertheless, and disturbing as it may be, it is clearly the case that there is a kind of "provisional" cosmic dualism within the New Testament: not an ultimate dualism, of course, between two equal principles; but certainly a conflict between a sphere of created autonomy that strives against God on the one hand and the saving love of God in time on the other. It is a patristic notion (developed with extraordinary profundity by Maximus the Confessor) that humanity was created as the *methorios* (the boundary or frontier) between the physical and the spiritual realms, or as the priesthood of creation that unites earth to heaven, and that thus, in the fall of man, all of material existence was made subject to the dominion of death. To say that God elects to fashion rational creatures in his image, and so grants them the freedom to bind themselves and the greater physical order to another master — to say that he who sealed up the doors of the sea might permit them to be opened again by another, more reckless hand — is not to say that God's ultimate design for his creatures can be thwarted. It is to acknowledge, however, that his will can be resisted by a real and (by his grace) autonomous force of defiance, or can be hidden from us by the history of cosmic corruption, and that the final realization of the good he intends in all things has the form (not simply as a dramatic fiction, for our edification or his glory, nor simply as a paedagogical device on his part, but in truth) of a divine victory.

The very word "world" *(kosmos)* appears in the New Testament with two quite distinct and even opposed meanings (this is especially the case in John's Gospel). At times it is a synonym for "creation" *(ktisis)* and so signifies

merely the handiwork of God and the object of his redemptive care: "God so loved the world that he gave his
only begotten Son. . . . God sent not his Son into the world
to condemn the world, but that the world through him
might be saved" (John 3:16-17); "I came not to judge the
world, but to save the world" (John 12:47). Even in its
bondage to death, the "cosmos" (in this sense of the word)
bears glorious testimony to the power and righteousness
of God: "For the invisible things of him from the creation
of the world are clearly seen, being understood by the
things that are made, even his eternal power and God-
head" (Rom. 1:20). But "world" is also used to indicate the
present "order" (the proper meaning of *kosmos*) that en-
slaves creation and that strives incessantly against God,
jealous of its plunder. When the incarnate God appears
within *this* "cosmos," it is to rescue the beauties of creation
from the torments of fallen nature, but it is also an act of
judgment and of conquest. Christ enters our reality as, of
course, the universal Logos through whom "all things consist" (Col. 1:17), but also as the stranger God who comes
"from above" (John 3:31; 8:23): "He was in the world, and
the world was made by him, and the world knew him not"
(John 1:10); neither he nor his Kingdom, he says, is "of this
world" (John 8:23; 17:14, 16; 18:36); this world hates him and
those he has chosen to raise "out of" it (John 15:18-19); "Be
of good cheer," he tells his apostles; "I have overcome the

world" (John 16:33). The "cosmos" (in this sense of the word) is an empire of cruelty, aggression, envy, misery, violence, falsehood, greed, ignorance, and spiritual desolation: it is death working in all things, the power to dominate or slay, but not to make new. It is that "present evil world" (Gal. 1:4) to which Paul says we must never be conformed (Rom. 12:2).

In the New Testament, our condition as fallen creatures is explicitly portrayed as a subjugation to the subsidiary and often mutinous authority of angelic and demonic "powers," which are not able to defeat God's transcendent and providential governance of all things, but which certainly are able to act against him within the limits of cosmic time. This age is ruled by spiritual and terrestrial "thrones, dominions, principalities, and powers" (Col. 1:16; cf. 1 Cor. 2:8; Eph. 1:21; 3:10), by "the elements *(stoicheia)* of the world" (Gal. 4:3), and by "the prince of the power of the air" (Eph. 2:2), who — while they cannot ultimately separate us from God's love (Rom. 8:38) — nevertheless contend against us: "For we wrestle not against flesh and blood, but against principalities, against powers, against the rulers of the darkness of this world, against spiritual wickedness in high places" (Eph. 6:12). Hence John's Gospel calls the devil "the prince of this world" (John 12:31; 14:30; 16:11), while 2 Corinthians calls him (somewhat shockingly) "the god of this world"

(2 Cor. 4:4), and 1 John says that "the whole world lies in the power of the evil one" (1 John 5:19). The cosmos, then, is divided between two kingdoms, that of God and that of death. And while God must triumph, death remains mighty and terrible until the end — it remains, in fact, the "last enemy that shall be destroyed" (1 Cor. 15:26).

Whatever one makes of this vision of things, it surely is no bland cosmic optimism. However one chooses to interpret the "powers," and indeed whether one believes in the Christian God or not, one must acknowledge that the solicitude shown by some Christians for *total* and *direct* divine sovereignty in all the eventualities of the fallen world is not shared by the authors of the New Testament canon. Much less is there anything to be found in Scripture remotely resembling theodicy's attempted moral justification of the present cosmic order. At the heart of the gospel, of course, is an ineradicable triumphalism, a conviction that the will of God cannot ultimately be defeated and that the victory over evil and death has already been won: "When he ascended up on high, he led captivity captive, and gave gifts unto men" (Eph. 4:8); "And having spoiled principalities and powers, he made a show of them openly, triumphing over them in it" (Col. 2:15). But it is also a victory, we are assured, that is yet to come. For now, we live amid a strife of darkness and light, falsehood and truth, death and life. This world remains a field where the wheat and the tares have been sown side by side, and so they must grow till the harvest comes (Matt. 13:38). Until then, as Paul says, all creation languishes in anguished anticipation of the day when God's glory will transfigure all things:

> For I reckon that the sufferings of the present time are not worthy to be compared with the glory which shall be revealed in us. For the earnest expectation of creation [*ktisis*] waiteth for the manifestation of the sons of God. For creation was made subject to vanity, not willingly, but by reason of him who subjected it, yet hoping that creation itself also shall be delivered by the bondage of corruption into the glorious liberty of the children of God. For we know that the whole creation groaneth and travaileth in pain together until now. (Rom. 8:18-22)

Whether or not one believes in such glory, or has faith in its final advent, or can in fact "see" it even now through the veil of death and our estrangement from God (though, I suspect, that all of us see it at times, whether our internal dispositions permit us to recognize what we see or not), one should be able to grasp that it is not a glory immediately revealed in cosmic or human history, but is rather one that appears before, alongside, within, and beyond that history, always present, yet also for now deferred, and so visible to us only "through a glass, darkly" (1 Cor. 13:12). This glory is not simply the hidden rationality of history, but a contrary history that pervades and that will finally overwhelm the world of our fallenness. It is not the sublime or sacred logic of nature, but what shines through the promise of nature's loveliness, a beauty of which nature as we now know it is only a spectral remnant or a delightful foretaste. This being so, there comes a point at which even Ivan Karamazov's agonies of conscience begin to look almost irrelevant: for they concern a God who has need of suffering and death, who "chooses" them as the instruments of a perfect and universal design that — but for them — could not be realized.

But, seen differently, as paradise laboring in subjection to evils that God has overthrown and will finally destroy, the world as we know it is not *simply* the work of one all-determining will. This is why Zosima's unashamedly unempirical vision of creation is a legitimate riposte to Ivan's doubt (even if it is not a refutation). As soon as one sheds the burden of the desire for total explanation — as soon as one has come to see the history of suffering as a contingency and an absurdity, in which grace is ever at work but upon which it does not depend, and has come also to see the promised end of all things not as the dialectical residue of a great cosmic and moral process, but as

68

something far more glorious than the pitiable resources of fallen time could ever yield — one is confronted with only this bare choice: either one embraces the mystery of created freedom and accepts that the union of free spiritual creatures with the God of love is a thing so wonderful that the power of creation to enslave itself to death must be permitted by God; or one judges that not even such rational freedom is worth the risk of a cosmic fall and the terrible injustice of the consequences that follow from it. But, then, since there can be no context in which such a judgment can be meaningfully made, no perspective from which a finite Euclidean mind can weigh eschatological glory in the balance against earthly suffering, the rejection of God on these grounds cannot really be a rational decision, but only a moral pathos.

And yet Ivan's argument still cannot be set aside, for a number of reasons: because it is in fact a genuinely *moral* pathos to which it gives expression, which means that it is haunted by the declaration in Christ of God's perfect goodness; and because it is precisely the finite Euclidean mind that is meant to be transfigured by God's love and awakened to God's mercy, and so the restlessness of the unquiet heart must not be treated as mere foolish unfaithfulness; and because, simply said, the suffering of children remains real and horrible and unjust, and it is obscene to seek to mitigate the scandal of such suffering by allowing hope to degenerate into banal confidence in "God's great plan." Anyway, such confidence all too easily blinds us to the spiritual universe of the New Testament. For the secret of Ivan's argument (as I have already hinted) is that it is not a challenge to Christian faith advanced from the position of unbelief; more subtly, it is a challenge to the habitual optimism or pagan fatalism or empty logical determinism of many Christians advanced from the position of a deeper, more original, more revolutionary, more "Christian" vision of God and understanding of evil. For behind Ivan's anguish lies an intuition — which is purely Christian, even if many Christians are insensible to it — that it is impossible for the infinite God of love directly or positively to *will* evil (physical or moral), even in a provisional or transitory way: and this because he is infinitely free.

III

Of course, we are inclined (especially today) to think of freedom wholly in terms of arbitrary or pathetic volition, a potency made actual every time one chooses a particular course of action out from a variety of other possibilities. And obviously, for finite intellects and wills, this is the minimal form that liberty must assume; but it is also, just as obviously, a form of subordination and confinement. All possible choices are external to the will that chooses; they shape it from without, defining it even before it has chosen. Moreover, these possibilities are exclusive of one another: one makes a possible course of action real by rendering other courses of action impossible. And, as we all know, one can choose foolishly, or maliciously, or with a divided will. Freedom, so understood, would consist in no more than a certain kind of largely vacuous and limited potentiality dependent upon other limited and limiting potentialities.

A higher understanding of human freedom, however, is inseparable from a definition of human nature. To be free is to be able to flourish as the kind of being one is, and so to attain the ontological good toward which one's nature is oriented; freedom is the unhindered realization of a complex nature in its proper end (natural and supernatural), and this is consummate liberty and happiness. The will that chooses poorly, then — through ignorance, maleficence, or corrupt desire — has not thereby become freer, but has further enslaved itself to those forces that prevent it from achieving its full expression. And it is this richer understanding of human freedom that provides us some analogy to the freedom of God. For God is infinite actuality, the source and end of all being, the eternally good, for whom mere arbitrary "choice" — as among pos-

sibilities that somehow exceed his "present" actuality —
would be a deficiency, a limitation placed upon his infinite power to be God. His freedom is the impossibility of
any force, pathos, or potentiality interrupting the perfection of his nature or hindering him in the realization of
his own illimitable goodness, in himself and in his creatures. To be "capable" of evil — to be able to do evil or to
be affected by an encounter with it — would in fact be an
incapacity in God; and to require evil to bring about his
good ends would make him less than the God he is. The
object of God's will is his own infinite goodness, and it is
an object perfectly realized, and so he is *free*.

This is a claim not only doctrinal but blatantly metaphysical, but this is no cause for tentativeness. Not only
are the speculative concerns of developed Christian phi-
losophy already substantially present in the Hellenistic
metaphysical motifs and assumptions that permeate the
New Testament (deny these though some might), but
classical Christian metaphysics, as elaborated from the
patristic through the high medieval periods, is a logically
necessary consequence of the gospel: both insofar as it
unfolds the inevitable ontological implications of Christian doctrines concerning the Trinity and creation *ex
nihilo;* and insofar also as Christianity's evangelical vocation requires believers to be able to articulate the inherent rationality of their faith. And high among Christian

tradition's most venerable and most indispensable metaphysical commitments is the definition of evil as a *steresis agathou* or *privatio boni,* a privation of the good, a purely parasitic corruption of created reality, possessing no essence or nature of its own. "God is light, and in him is no darkness at all" (1 John 1:5); and as he is the source of all things, the fountainhead of being, everything that exists partakes of his goodness and is therefore, in its essence, entirely good.

Evil is born in the will: it consists not in some other separate thing standing alongside the things of creation, but is only a shadow, a turning of the hearts and minds of rational creatures away from the light of God back toward the nothingness from which all things are called. This is not to say that evil is then somehow illusory; it is only to say that evil, rather than being a discrete substance, is instead a kind of ontological wasting disease. Born of nothingness, seated in the rational will that unites material and spiritual creation, it breeds a contagion of nothingness throughout the created order. Death works its ruin in all things, all minds are darkened, all desires are invaded by selfishness, weakness, rapacity, and the *libido dominandi* — the lust to dominate — and thus tend away from the beauty of God indwelling his creatures and toward the deformity of nonbeing. To say otherwise would involve either denying God's transcendence (by suggesting that he is not the source of all being) or denying his goodness (by suggesting that good and evil alike participate in the being that flows from him, and that his nature must therefore be beyond the distinction between them).

Hence evil can have no proper role to play in God's determination of himself or purpose for his creatures, even if by economy God can bring good from evil; it can in no way supply any imagined deficiency in God's or creation's goodness; it has no "contribution" to make. Being infinitely sufficient in himself, God has no need of a passage through sin and death to manifest his glory in his creatures, or to join them perfectly to himself, or to elevate their minds to the highest possible vision of the riches of his nature. This is why it is misleading even to say, as did that scholar mentioned above, that the drama of fall and redemption will make the final state of things more glorious than it might otherwise have been. There is precedent for such a view in Catholic tradition, admittedly — even Aquinas seems perhaps to grant that it might be so — but the idea is incoherent. It would entail the conclusion either that there are certain ends that God can accomplish in his creatures only by way of evil (which grants evil substance and makes God its cause) or that God chooses to reward transgression with greater blessings as a demonstration of his sovereignty (which means

that he is unjust or that his righteousness is divided
against itself or that his original prohibition of sin was a
kind of lie; and perhaps also means that evil is something
real that he confronts and to which he reacts like a finite
subject). No less metaphysically confused — though immeasurably more disconcerting — is the suggestion of
that junior professor that God requires suffering and
death to reveal certain of his attributes, which is false for
much the same reasons. (And, surely, one should really
say that it is precisely sin, suffering, and death that blind
us to God's true nature.)

Intimately associated with the doctrine of the *privatio
boni* is the equally necessary doctrine of divine *apatheia*
or impassibility, the teaching that God is, in his nature,
impervious to any external force of change — any pathos
or affect — and is free of all reactive or changing emo-
tions. This teaching has never, it must be stressed, denied
the full reality of Christ's suffering on the cross: inasmuch
as the divine Word truly became man, and inasmuch as
there is but one Person or hypostasis in Christ, God the
Word has experienced pain and death in their fullest
depth. The teaching merely affirms two logically necessary truths. First, that susceptibility to suffering (which is
a limitation, not a capacity) is a natural property of
Christ's humanity, not his divinity, which fact does not in
any fashion endanger the unity of Christ (since it is not

one's "nature" that is the subject of any experience, but one's person, and so logically it is indeed the divine Word who suffered). And, second, that the experience of the cross does not alter or "improve" or "add" to the infinite God: he did not need to learn to love us, and suffering and death are privations of reality, not "new realities" of which God needs to be "apprised."

Some theologians, acting I suspect from a somewhat superficial understanding of the doctrine, have wished at times to reject *apatheia* as an alien import from Greek metaphysics. But it is not, I would assert, a negotiable doctrine: the very rationality of the gospel requires it. This is not to ignore the anxiety that the word "impassibility" can occasion; for some, it seems to suggest a God who is "unfeeling" (in the colloquial sense) and therefore "uncaring." And obviously it is difficult for us to avoid imagining God in terms of finite psychological subjectivity, and so thinking of him as someone who "experiences" a reality set over against him, and who therefore knows things by way of contrasts and limits. When we allow this habit of thought to become something like an intellectual conviction, however, we become guilty of both an infantile anthropomorphism and a philosophical catachresis. This is especially true when we think of God as requiring "passions" to love us, as loving us "responsively," as indeed "needing" us. No doubt such language gives us a sense of our own significance, and certainly it accords with our own experiences of love; but it also effectively denies the transcendence of God and the plenitude of his charity. In fact, it dissembles the very nature of love; for love is not — in its inmost essence — a reaction. In God, who is its transcendent origin and end, it is the one infinite and changeless act of being that makes all else actual, and so is purely positive, sufficient in itself, and without any need of contrariety to be fully vital and creative. As Trinity, God always already possesses the fullness of charity in himself — difference and regard, feasting and fellowship, perfect delight and perfect rest — and has no need of any external pathos to waken or fecundate his love. We are not necessary to him: he is not nourished by our sacrifices or ennobled by our virtues, any more than he is diminished by our sins and sufferings. This is a truth that may not aggrandize us, but it does, more wonderfully, glorify us: for it means that, though he had no need of us, still he loved us when we were not. And this is why love, in its divine depth, is *apatheia.*

The failure to embrace the idea of divine impassibility becomes especially disastrous for Christians when it causes them to think of the crucifixion as an event in the genesis of God's personality, a trial through which he passed as our fellow sufferer so that he could achieve in himself the perfection of self-abandoning love. At its most vulgar, this way of thinking implies that God took our suffering into himself as something that changed or enlarged his knowledge of us, and it implies also that on the cross he had to learn the extent of our suffering: now, perhaps, he understands what we must endure. This is simply nonsense. It is a logical absurdity simultaneously to assert that God is the source of all that is *and* that God can "become" something more or other than he previously was. To suggest that God becomes the God he is by suffering passions, according to encounters with other and tragic realities (even if he creates those realities), is to trade in mythology, to preach a finite God, one who is no doubt a "supreme being" but not the source of all being. And if God's love were in any sense shaped by sin, suffering, and death, then sin, suffering, and death would always be in some sense features of who he is. This not only means that evil would be a distinct reality over against God, and God's love something inherently deficient and reactive; it also means that evil would be somehow a part of God, and that goodness would require evil to be good. Such a God could not *be* love, even if in some sense he should prove to be "loving." Nor would he be the good as such, nor being as such. He, like us, would be a synthesis of death and life.

All of this must be kept in mind when one reflects upon the relation between Christ's sacrifice upon the cross and the suffering of creation. One clear pattern that emerged from the tangled thicket of responses provoked by my *Wall Street Journal* column on the Indian Ocean tsunami was, among my Catholic interlocutors, a strong and (to my mind) theologically healthy emphasis upon our participation in Christ's redemptive suffering, in keeping with Colossians 1:24 ("[I] now rejoice in my sufferings for you, and fill up that which is lacking of the afflictions of Christ in my flesh, for the sake of his body, which is the Church"), and upon the way in which the mystical body of Christ is sustained and fortified by suffering borne together and on behalf of others and — in imitation of Christ — without despair or hatred. But there was also a tendency (which may have had more to do with the speed with which the conversation evolved than anything else) to make this lovely doctrine sound like a comprehensive explanation and rationalization of all earthly suffering, which it most definitely is not.

For one thing, it seems oddly imperious to impose such an explanation upon the sufferings of those who are not Christian (as were most of the victims of the Indian Ocean tsunami), or upon the sufferings of those who throughout the ages have lived and died apart from any knowledge of Jesus of Nazareth, or for that matter upon the sufferings of animals. Yes, such things evoke compassion and service from Christian hearts, in whatsoever measure is possible; but that certainly does not make those sufferings somehow wholly meaningful and therefore unscandalous. The cross of Christ is not, after all, simply an eternal validation of pain and death, but their overthrow. If all the tribulations of this world were to be written off as calculably *necessary* contributions to redemption — part of the great "balance" of things — then Christ's sacrifice would not be a unique saving act so much as the metaphysical ground for a universe of "sacrifice," wherein suffering and death are part of the sublime and inevitable fabric of finitude; and divine providence would be indistinguishable from fate. We would find ourselves standing again upon the Kuru plain (where I think, to be fair, even the Bhaktic piety of the *Gita* would not be content to leave us). Again, such was not the intention of my interlocutors. But one must be careful to draw a clear distinction in one's language between a recognition of our gracious participation in Christ's unique victory over death and any attempt to conscript death into a perfect alliance with God's saving action in history.

This is one reason why such thoroughly speculative principles as the *privatio boni* and divine *apatheia* are of such crucial doctrinal importance as well: they remind us how radically we must understand the sacrifice of Christ on the cross not as an act of divine impotence but of divine power. The cross most definitely is not an instance of God submitting himself to an irresistible force so as to define himself in his struggle with nothingness or so as to be "rescued" from his impassibility by becoming our fellow sufferer; but neither is it a vehicle whereby God reconciles either himself or us to death. Rather, he subverts death, and makes a way through it to a new life. The cross is thus a triumph of divine *apatheia,* limitless and immutable love sweeping us up into itself, taking all suffering and death upon itself without being changed, modified, or defined by it, and so destroying its power and making us, by participation in Christ, "more than conquerors" (Rom. 8:37). God does not simply submit himself to the cycle of natural necessity or to the dialectic of historical necessity but shatters the power of both, and thereby overthrows the ancient principalities, the immemorial empire of death. Easter utterly confounds the "rulers of this age" (1 Cor. 2:8), and in fact reverses the verdict they have pronounced upon Christ, thereby revealing that the cosmic, sacred, political, and civic powers of all who condemn Christ have become tyranny, falsehood, and injustice. Easter is an act of "rebellion" against all false necessity and all illegitimate or misused authority, all cruelty and heartless chance. It liberates us from servitude to and terror before the "elements." It emancipates us from fate. It overcomes the "world." Easter should make rebels of us all.

IV

What then, one might well ask, *is* divine providence? Certainly all Christians must affirm God's transcendent governance of everything, even fallen history and fallen nature, and must believe that by that governance he will defeat evil and bring the final good of all things out of the darkness of "this age." It makes a considerable difference, however — nothing less than our understanding of the nature of God is at stake — whether one says that God has eternally willed the history of sin and death, and all that comes to pass therein, as the proper or necessary means of achieving his ends, or whether one says instead that God has willed his good in creatures from eternity and will bring it to pass, despite their rebellion, by so ordering all things toward his goodness that even evil (which he does not cause) becomes an occasion of the operations of grace. And it is only the latter view than can accurately be called a doctrine of "providence" in the properly theological sense; the former view is mere determinism.

God has fashioned creatures in his image so that they might be joined in a perfect union with him in the rational freedom of love. For that very reason, what God permits, rather than violate the autonomy of the created world, may be *in itself* contrary to what he wills. But there is no contradiction in saying that, in his omniscience, omnipotence, and transcendence of time, God can both allow created freedom its scope and yet so constitute the world that nothing can prevent him from bringing about the beatitude of his Kingdom. Indeed we must say this: as God did not will the fall, and yet always wills all things toward himself, the entire history of sin and death is in an ultimate sense a pure contingency, one that is not as such desired by God, but that is nevertheless constrained by providence to serve his transcendent purpose. God does not will evil in the sinner. Neither does he will that the sinner should perish (2 Peter 3:9; Ezek. 33:11). He does not place evil in the heart. He does not desire the convulsive reign of death in nature. But neither will he suffer defeat in these things.

Providence works at the level of what Aquinas would call primary causality: that is, it is so transcendent of the operation of secondary causes — which is to say, finite and contingent causes immanent to the realm of created things — that it can at once create freedom and also assure that no consequence of the misuse of that freedom will prevent him from accomplishing the good he intends in all things. This is the same as saying that the transcendent act of creation, though it grants existence to creatures out of the plenitude of God's being, nonetheless brings forth beings that are genuinely other than God, without there being any "conflict" between his infinite actuality and their contingent participation in it. As God is the source and end of all being, nothing that is can be completely alienated from him; all things exist by virtue of being called from nothingness toward his goodness; every instance of finite becoming or thought or desire subsists in the creature's "ecstasy" out of nonbeing and into the infinite splendor of God. And it is for just this reason that providence does not and cannot in any way betray the true freedom of the creature: every free movement of the will is possible only by virtue of the more primordial longing of all things for the beauty of God (to borrow the language of Maximus the Confessor, our "gnomic will" depends upon our "natural will"), and so every free act — even the act of hating God — arises from and is sustained by a more original love of God. It is impossible to desire anything without implicitly desiring the infinite source of all things; even the desire of the suicide for the peace of oblivion is born of a love of self — however tragically distorted it has become — that is itself born of a deeper love for the God from whom the self comes and to whom the self is called.

This original vocation of the creature — which is the very ground of our existence — is heaven in us, and indeed hell. As Zosima tells Alyosha (again following Isaac the Syrian and a larger Eastern Christian mystical tradition), what we call hell is nothing but the rage and remorse of the soul that will not yield itself to love. The natural will must return to God, no matter what, but if the freedom of the gnomic will refuses to open itself to the mercy and glory of God, the wrathful soul experiences the transfiguring and deifying fire of love not as bliss but as chastisement and despair. The highest freedom and happiness of the creature (in keeping with the definition of freedom given above) is the perfection of the creature's nature in union with God. And the highest work of providential grace is to set our deepest, "natural" will free from everything (even the abuse of our freedom) that would separate us from that end, all the time preserving the dignity of the divine image within us.

Providence, then — and this is what it is most important to grasp — is not the same thing as a universal teleology. To believe in divine and unfailing providence is not to burden one's conscience with the need to see every event in this world not only as an occasion of God's grace, but as a positive determination of God's will whereby he brings to pass a comprehensive design that, in the absence of any single one of these events, would not have been possible. It may seem that this is to draw only the finest of logical distinctions, one so fine indeed as to amount to little more than a sophistry. Some theologians — Calvin, for instance — have denied that the distinction between what God wills and what he permits has any meaning at all. And certainly there is no unanimity in the history of Christian exegesis on this matter. Certain classic Western interpretations of Paul's treatment of the hardening of Pharaoh's heart and of the hardened heart of Israel in Romans 9 have taken it as a clear statement of God's immediate determination of his creatures' wills. But in the Eastern Christian tradition, and in the thought of many of the greatest Western theologians, the same argument has often been understood to assert no more than that God in either case allowed a prior corruption of the will to run its course, or even — like a mire in the light of the sun — to harden before the outpouring of God's fiery mercy, and always for the sake of a greater good that will perhaps redound even to the benefit of the sinner. One might read Christ's answer to his disciples' question regarding why a man had been born blind — "that the works of God should be made manifest in him" (John 9:3) — either as a refutation or as a confirmation of the distinction between divine will and permission. When all is said and done, however, not only is the distinction neither illogical nor slight; it is an absolute necessity if — setting aside, as we should, all other judgments as suppositious, stochastic, and secondary — we are to be guided by the full character of what is revealed of God in Christ. For, after all, if it is from Christ that we are to learn how

God relates himself to sin, suffering, evil, and death, it would seem that he provides us little evidence of anything other than a regal, relentless, and miraculous enmity: sin he forgives, suffering he heals, evil he casts out, and death he conquers. And absolutely nowhere does Christ act as if any of these things are part of the eternal work or purposes of God.

Which it is well to remember. For somehow the most vital and urgent thing to know about the God revealed in the Gospels is that (for instance) the tears of that little girl suffering in the dark of whom Ivan speaks are not a reflection of the divine will or a necessary moment in the dialectical unfolding of history — according to God's "great plan" — toward the "kingdom" that awaits it as a kind of immanent cosmic telos. God may permit evil to have a history of its own so as not to despoil creatures of their destiny of free union with him in love, but he is not the sole and irresistible agency shaping that history according to eternal arbitrary decrees. Thomas Aquinas — who did most definitely insist upon a distinction between divine will and divine permission — stated the logic of providence with elegant brevity: *Deus plus amat quod est magis bonum, et ideo magis vult praesentiam magis boni quam absentiam minus mali:* "God loves more the greater good — and thus more greatly wills the presence of the greater good — than he does the absence of the lesser

evil." Of course, Ivan would not in all likelihood be molli-
fied by such language. Is it indeed, after all, only a "lesser
evil" — as compared to any imaginable "greater good" —
that that little girl endured such torments? Is not this an
evil so immense and irreconcilable that it is fixed in the
heart of eternity, an everlasting indictment of divine
mercy and refutation of divine justice?

Perhaps there is no compelling answer to this, at least
not one that can be put into words. Either one "sees" that
glory or one does not — believes in it or cannot — and in
either case one may be moved by a love of the good. But,
whether one has faith or not, the moment the specters of
absolute teleology and insipid metaphysical optimism
have been exorcised, a genuine hope in the subtle workings of saving grace becomes possible — intellectually
and morally. And, this being so, one should also observe
that there is a sense in which Ivan's love of that little girl is
always in danger of becoming a kind of demonic compassion: a desire that she not exist at all, a conviction that it
were better she had never been summoned into the
wounded freedom of cosmic time or called to rational
union with God than that she suffer the wrongs done her
at the hands of fallen creatures. Here one might even suspect Ivan of a willingness then to freeze her forever in the
darkness of her torments — as a perpetual symbol of his
revolt against heaven — rather than release her into a

happiness that he thinks unjust. For Christians, though, to be is the first good, the first gift of God's gratuitous love, and the highest good is to be joined to God in the free movement of the soul. But, again, to believe in the infinite goodness of being, one must be able to see it; and this no mere argument can bring about.

The moral rationality of Ivan's rebellion remains entirely unassailable, however, when it is set against those forms of theological fatalism that, having failed to understand the difference between primary and secondary — or transcendent and immanent — causality, defame the love and goodness of God out of a servile and unhealthy fascination with his "dread sovereignty." The crude and unapologetic "double predestinarianism" of Gottschalk in the ninth century provides a particularly acute example. And there could scarcely be any better evidence of what mischief can be worked upon theological thinking when the difference between primary and secondary causality is forgotten than the heresy of "limited atonement," which has so dreadfully disfigured certain streams of traditional Reformed thought. The doctrine, of course, completely contradicts Scripture: "And he is the propitiation for our sins: and not for ours only, but also for the sins of the whole world" (1 John 2:2). And the assertion sometimes made by proponents of the doctrine that all biblical statements of God's universal will to salvation in fact refer only to his will for the elect is entirely incongruent with the language of 1 Timothy 2:4, which clearly states that God desires that "all human beings [*pantas anthropous*] should be saved and come to a knowledge of the truth." But, when any meaningful difference between will and permission has been excluded, and when the transcendent causality of the creator God has been confused with the immanent web of causation that constitutes the world of our experiences, it becomes impossible to imagine that what God wills might not be immediately convertible with what occurs in time; and thus both the authority of Scripture and the justice of God must fall before the inexorable logic of absolute divine sovereignty.

At its most unfortunate, this exaggerated adoration of God's sheer omnipotence can yield conclusions as foolish as Calvin's assertion, in Book III of the *Institutes,* that God predestined the fall of man so as to show forth his greatness in both the salvation and the damnation of those he has eternally preordained to their several fates. Were this so, God would be the author of and so entirely beyond both good and evil, or at once both and neither, or indeed merely evil (which power without justice always is). The curious absurdity of all such doctrines is that, out of a pious anxiety to defend God's transcendence against any scintilla of genuine creaturely freedom, they threaten effectively to collapse that transcendence into absolute identity — with the world, with us, with the devil. For, unless the world is truly set apart from God and possesses a dependent but real liberty of its own analogous to the freedom of God, everything is merely a fragment of divine volition, and God is simply the totality of all that is and all that happens; there is no creation, but only an oddly pantheistic expression of God's unadulterated power. One wonders, indeed, if a kind of reverse Prometheanism does not lurk somewhere within such a theology, a refusal on the part of the theologian to be a creature, a desire rather to be dissolved into the infinite fiery flood of God's solitary and arbitrary act of will. In any event, such a God, being nothing but will willing itself, would be no more than an infinite tautology — the sovereignty of glory displaying itself in the glory of sovereignty — and so an infinite banality.

This is why I say that, within Ivan's arraignment of God's design in creation, one can hear the suppressed but still prophetic voice of a deeper, truer, more radical and revolutionary Christianity. For if indeed there were a God whose true nature — whose justice or sovereignty — were revealed in the death of a child or the dereliction of a soul or a predestined hell, then it would be no great transgression to think of him as a kind of malevolent or contemptible demiurge, and to hate him, and to deny him worship, and to seek a better God than he. But Christ has overthrown all those principalities that rule without justice and in defiance of charity, and has cast out the god of this world; and so we are free (even now, in this mortal body) from slavery to arbitrary power, from fear of hell's dominion, and from any superstitious subservience to fate. And this is the holy liberty — the gospel — that lies hidden but active in the depths of Ivan's rebellion.

V

I said at the beginning of this book that silence might have been the wisest response in the days following the Indian Ocean catastrophe. And here, after (at this writing) two months and many thousands of words, I remain uncertain whether what I have said is proper or even remotely adequate. These rather desultory reflections were occasioned by what happened on that day, but I have clearly ventured far from any direct discussion of the sufferings of those who fell victim to that horrendous paroxysm of nature at her most murderous; and I do not know if I ought to have done so. This has not, obviously, been a book of apologetics, in large part because I still find myself less perturbed by the sanctimonious condescension of many of those who do not believe than by either the gelid dispassion or the shapeless sentimentality of certain of those who do. Neither has it been a book of "technical" or "philosophical" theology, though I have at points touched upon "technical" elements of Christian philosophical tradition (too lightly, I fear, to be entirely convincing and too heavily to be entirely lucid). Much less has it been a book of consolations. Rather, my principal aim has simply been to elucidate — as far as in me lies — what I understand to be the true scriptural account of God's goodness, the shape of redemption, the nature of evil, and the conditions of a fallen world, not to convince anyone of its credibility, but simply to show where many of the arguments of Christianity's antagonists and champions alike fail to address what is most essential to the gospel.

Clearly, also, I have expended at least as much energy contending against what I take to be defective formulations of Christian faith as I have against skeptical assaults upon that faith, but this is because, generally speaking, the latter have so little relevance to the object of their hostility that they pose no very formidable menace. It may seem, especially at the end of my reflections, that I have made Calvinism into my particular *bête noire,* though that was never my intention. In part, this merely reflects the reality that, after the appearance of my column, those among its critics who exhibited the most exuberant callousness regarding the dead — even all those tens of thousands of dead children — and who reacted with the greatest belligerence and most violent vituperation to any suggestion that God might not be the immediate cause of all evil in the world were all Calvinists of a particularly rigorist persuasion. So the shape of the debate was to some degree laid out for me in advance. It also reflects, however, the reality that between Eastern Orthodox and Reformed theology there are some differences so vast that no reconciliation is possible. And I would be lying if I denied that, in many of the broad themes of the theology of Calvin, there is something in my view terribly amiss and extremely remote from the genuine theology of the New Testament (but he was, after all, working within a certain venerable tradition of exegesis). All that said, I do know that there is far more to Calvin's thought than a pure predestinarianism. I only wish it had been historically possible for him (and for other of his contemporaries) to take the subtleties of high scholastic theology more seriously, and the riches of patristic thought more to heart.

What might seem most offensively or perhaps risibly eccentric about this book, to certain theologically literate readers at least, is the subtle (or not so subtle) current of what looks like a slight sympathy for Gnosticism running through it. I admit that it is my conviction that there are certain notable respects in which ancient Gnosticism was far nearer to the religious vision of the New Testament than are many now well-established forms of Christian belief (which does not of course preclude the opposite also being true). If nothing else, the Gnostics of the early centuries inhabited the same imaginative and spiritual universe as the earliest Christians: they no more than Paul took the principalities and powers and elements of this world as myths or allegories; they no less than Paul proclaimed themselves free from the tyranny of the "god of this world." And, like Paul or the author of John's Gospel, the Gnostics understood spiritual liberation as something subversive of the order of "this cosmos," a manumission from the sway of the ancient terrestrial and celestial powers, a glorious *escape* from the kingdom of death. Any Christian who has not felt at least an occasional stirring of the pathos of Gnosticism — at the thought, for instance, of a small girl weeping in torment in the darkness — and of a rage against the fashion of this world, and of a mysterious yearning for another and perfect world, at once strange and familiar, cannot in all likelihood fully appreciate the spiritual and moral sensibility of the New Testament.

But slight sympathy should not be mistaken for profound admiration. Despite the brave attempts of some of Gnosticism's modern apologists to treat its various systems as ingenious allegories, Gnosticism's chief distinc-

tions (apart from its visible streak of adolescent callousness toward those who are not among the elect) were its
lack of metaphysical sophistication, its consequent reli-
ance upon absurd mythologies, and the philosophically
incoherent dualism to which these things led. There is
nothing in the literary remains of Gnosticism that approaches the subtlety, speculative profundity, or sym-
bolic genius of the Gospel of John, for instance, nothing
that demonstrates any awareness of the logically necessary *unity* of being, no hint of an understanding that everything that exists must flow from the same creative
source, the same transcendent Logos, and must therefore
be essentially good and inalienable from the God who
made it. The New Testament, animated by just this
knowledge, offers an intellectually rigorous and spiritually profound vision of this world as at once *ktisis* and
kosmos, God's good creation and fallen nature, a realm of
spiritual struggle between the natural and gnomic wills
of rational creation. In place of this the Gnostics, through
manifest philosophical ineptitude, could offer nothing
but childish and unbearably boring fantasies.

What looks like a sympathy for Gnosticism in these
pages, then, is more truly a prejudice in favor of the New
Testament's cosmological and soteriological imagery.
Modern Christians may understandably have little
knowledge of or taste for the angelology or demonology

96

of the early church, but this does not excuse them from grasping how radically the gospel is pervaded by a sense that the brokenness of the fallen world is the work of rebellious rational free will, which God permits its reign, and pervaded also by a sense that Christ comes genuinely to *save* creation, to conquer, to rescue, to defeat the power of evil in all things. This great narrative of fall and redemption is not a charade, not simply a dramaturgical lesson regarding God's absolute prerogatives prepared for us from eternity, but a real consequence of the mystery of created freedom and the fullness of grace. For, at the end of the day, the crude dualism of the Gnostics springs from the same philosophical failing as does the most unsophisticated theological monism of divine will: the failure to see how God's act of being — through its infinity and transcendence — can make room in itself for the real being of finite creatures without thereby being diminished, and how therefore God's freedom — through its infinity and transcendence — can make room in its determinations for the real freedom of finite rational wills without thereby being weakened or compromised. All of this, however, is matter for a much longer and more elaborate book than this. At the moment it is enough simply to make this point clear: God's gracious will for his creatures — his willing of all things to his own infinite goodness — is the creative power that makes all things to be and the consummate happiness to which all things are called; but this does not (indeed, must not) mean that everything that happens is merely a direct expression of God's desire for his creatures or an essential stage within the divine plan for history.

There are those for whom saying this leaves behind an intolerable remainder, a kind of irrational surd. For them, unless one believes that every event has a substantial and organic (not merely accidental or occasional) place in the plot of universal history, and a specific function in the final synthesis of history at the end of time, then somehow the logical coherence of the universe begins to disintegrate, and God's final resolution of the story of the world is little more than a vulgar *deus ex machina*. But, of course, nothing is lost: the coherence of the universe is preserved by God acting to save what he has made — what is real, what has substance — not by providing a divine rationale for every dimension of every event in which his creatures are involved, no matter how much those events might reflect that ultimate privation, evil. There is, of course, some comfort to be derived from the thought that everything that occurs at the level of secondary causality — in nature or history — is governed not only by a transcendent providence but by a universal teleology that makes every instance of pain and loss an indispensable moment in a grand scheme whose ultimate synthesis will justify all things. But one should consider the price at which that comfort is purchased: it requires us to believe in and love a God whose good ends will be realized not only in spite of — but entirely by way of — every cruelty, every fortuitous misery, every catastrophe, every betrayal, every sin the world has ever known; it requires us to believe in the eternal spiritual necessity of a child dying an agonizing death from diphtheria, of a young mother ravaged by cancer, of tens of thousands of Asians swallowed in an instant by the sea, of millions murdered in death camps and gulags and forced famines (and so on). It is a strange thing indeed to seek peace in a universe rendered morally intelligible at the cost of a God rendered morally loathsome.

Or, to phrase all of this somewhat differently, words we would not utter to ease another's grief we ought not to speak to satisfy our own sense of piety. In the *New York Times* this morning, on this the last day I have set aside for the writing of this book, there appeared a report from Sri Lanka recounting, in part, the story of a large man of enormous physical strength who was unable to prevent four of his five children from perishing in the tsunami, and who — as he recited the names of his lost children to the reporter, in descending order of age, ending with the name of his four-year-old son — was utterly overwhelmed by his own weeping. Only a moral cretin at that

moment would have attempted to soothe his anguish by
assuring him that his children had died as a result of
God's eternal, inscrutable, and righteous counsels, and
that in fact their deaths had mysteriously served God's
purposes in history, and that all of this was completely
necessary for God to accomplish his ultimate design in
having created this world. Most of us would have the
good sense to be ashamed to speak such words; we would
recognize that they would offer no more credible comfort
than the vaporings of the most idiotically complacent
theodicy, and we would detest ourselves for giving voice
to odious banalities and blasphemous flippancies.

And this should tell us something. For if we would
think it shamefully foolish and cruel to say such things in
the moment when another's sorrow is most real and irre-
sistibly painful, then we ought never to say them; because what would still our tongues would be the knowledge (which we would possess at the time, though we
might forget it later) that such sentiments would amount
not only to an indiscretion or words spoken out of sea-
son, but to a vile stupidity and a lie told principally for
our own comfort, by which we would try to excuse ourselves for believing in an omnipotent and benevolent
God. In the process, moreover, we would be attempting
to deny that man a knowledge central to the gospel: the
knowledge of the evil of death, its intrinsic falsity, its un-

just dominion over the world, its ultimate nullity; the knowledge that God is not pleased or nourished by our deaths, that he is not the secret architect of evil, that he is the conqueror of hell, that he has condemned all these things by the power of the cross; the knowledge that God is life and light and infinite love, and that the path that leads through nature and history to his Kingdom does not simply follow the contours of either nature or history, or obey the logic immanent to them, but is opened to us by way of the natural and historical absurdity — or outrage — of the empty tomb.

However — fortunately, I think — we Christians are not obliged (and perhaps are not even allowed) to look upon the devastation of that day — to look, that is, upon the entire littoral rim of the Andaman Sea and Bay of Bengal and upper Indian Ocean strewn with tens of thousands of corpses, a third of them children — and to attempt to console ourselves or others with vacuous cant about the ultimate meaning or purpose residing in all that misery. Ours is, after all, a religion of salvation. Our faith is in a God who has come to rescue his creation from the absurdity of sin, the emptiness and waste of death, the forces — whether calculating malevolence or imbecile chance — that shatter living souls; and so we are permitted to hate these things with a perfect hatred. And we are not only permitted but required to believe that cosmic time as we know it, through all the immensity of its geological ages and historical epochs, is only a shadow of true time, and this world only a shadow of the fuller, richer, more substantial, more glorious creation that God intends; and to believe also that all of nature is a shattered mirror of divine beauty, still full of light, but riven by darkness. That ours is a fallen world is not, of course, a truth demonstrable to those who do not believe: it is not a first principle of faith, but rather something revealed to us only by what we know of Christ, in the light cast back from his saving action in history upon the whole of time. The fall of rational creation and the subjection of the cosmos to death is something that appears to us nowhere within the unbroken time of nature or history; we cannot search it out within the closed continuum of the wounded world; it belongs to another frame of time, another *kind* of time, one more real than the time of death.

When, however, we learn in Christ the nature of our first estate, and the divine destiny to which we are called, we begin to see — more clearly the more we are able to look upon the world with the eye of charity — that there is in all the things of earth a hidden glory waiting to be revealed, more radiant than a million suns, more beautiful than the most generous imagination or most ardent desire can now conceive. Or, rather, it is a glory not entirely hidden: veiled, rather, but shining in and through and upon all things. The imperishable goodness of all being does in fact show itself in all that is. It shows itself in the vast waters of the Indian Ocean, and it is not hard to see when those waters are silver and azure under the midday sky, or gold and indigo in the light of the setting sun, or jet and pearl in the light of the moon, and when their smoothly surging tides break upon the shore and harmlessly recede. But it is still there even when — the doors of the sea having broken their seals — those waters become suddenly dull and opaque with gray or sallow silt and rise up to destroy and kill without will or thought or purpose or mercy. At such times, to see the goodness indwelling all creation requires a labor of vision that only a faith in Easter can sustain; but it is there, effulgent, unfading, innocent, but languishing in bondage to corruption, groaning in anticipation of a glory yet to be revealed, both a promise of the Kingdom yet to come and a portent of its beauty.

Until that final glory, however, the world remains divided between two kingdoms, where light and darkness, life and death grow up together and await the harvest. In such a world, our portion is charity, and our sustenance is faith, and so it will be until the end of days. As for comfort, when we seek it, I can imagine none greater than the happy knowledge that when I see the death of a child, I do not see the face of God but the face of his enemy. Such faith might never seem credible to someone like Ivan Karamazov, or still the disquiet of his conscience, or give him peace in place of rebellion, but neither is it a faith that his arguments can defeat: for it is a faith that set us free from optimism long ago and taught us hope instead. Now we are able to rejoice that we are saved not through the immanent mechanisms of history and nature, but by grace; that God will not unite all of history's many strands in one great synthesis, but will judge much of history false and damnable; that he will not simply reveal the sublime logic of fallen nature, but will strike off the fetters in which creation languishes; and that, rather than showing us how the tears of a small girl suffering in the dark were necessary for the building of the Kingdom, he will instead raise her up and wipe away all tears from her eyes — and there shall be no more death, nor sorrow, nor crying, nor any more pain, for the former things will have passed away, and he that sits upon the throne will say, "Behold, I make all things new."

Bibliographical Note

Most of the information found in 1/I concerning the geol-
ogy of the northeastern Indian Ocean region and the history of the eruption of Krakatoa was gleaned from Simon
Winchester's fascinating and elegantly written *Krakatoa:
The Day the World Exploded: August 27, 1883,* published by
HarperCollins in 2003. The text of Voltaire's *Poëme sur le
désastre de Lisbonne* that I consulted for 1/III is found in
volume eight of the 1866 edition of the *Œuvres Complètes*
published in forty-six volumes by the Libraire de
L. Hachette et Ci^e, not because it is any more trustworthy
than the modern *Pléiade* edition, but simply because that
is the edition of Voltaire's works that I happen to possess. I
do not believe that the text of the poem differs in any notable respect between the two editions (with the excep-
tion, perhaps, of the pleasantly archaic diacritical mark
that bedizens the word *poëme* in the earlier edition and

that I retain out of instinctive atavism). In *The Brothers Karamazov,* Ivan's conversation with Alyosha (1/v) appears in Part Two, Book V, chs. 3-5.

The quotation from Aquinas in 2/I regarding the angelic governance of the material world appears in the *Summa Theologiae* I, q. 110, a. 1, corp., and the lines from Melville are from ch. 36 of *Moby Dick.* The passage from Bonaventure in 2/II is found in the *Itinerarium Mentis In Deum,* I, 15. The lines from Traherne come from the *Centuries* I:18, 27-31; I cite the text as it appears in Thomas Traherne, *Selected Poems and Prose,* published by Penguin Classics in 1991. Zosima's spiritual discourses appear in Part Two, Book VI, ch. 3 of *The Brothers Karamazov.* Isaac of Syria's celebrated description of the merciful heart comes from the eighty-first of his *Ascetical Homilies,* the only complete edition of which in English (as far as I am aware) was published by Holy Transfiguration Monastery in 1985, though the version that appears here is my own. Maximus the Confessor's teachings on the cultivation of charity can be found in *The Four Centuries on Charity,* which exists in at least two English translations: one issued by Newman Press in 1955 and one issued by Paulist Press (in *Selected Writings*) in 1985. The best summary of of his metaphysics of the divine Logos and created logoi is found in his seventh *Ambiguum,* the only English translation of which appears in a collection called

Bibliographical Note

On the Cosmic Mystery of Jesus Christ, released by St. Vladimir's Seminary Press in 2003.

As for my discussion of divine impassibility (2/III), I appreciate that I have not provided a particularly compelling or elaborate case for the doctrine here; I have accorded the topic a far fuller treatment in other places, especially in an article entitled "No Shadow of Turning: On Divine Impassibility" (*Pro Ecclesia*, Spring 2002). Aquinas's suggestion that God might permit sin so as to raise us to some higher good is found in the *Summa Theologiae* III, q. 1, a. 3, ad 3 (a theologically disappointing article, as it happens, in every respect); whether his remarks would apply, though, to the final state of the soul that enjoys the beatific vision is not entirely clear, since that is not the actual issue under discussion. Zosima's remarks on hell (2/IV) are found in his discourses, as above, and Isaac's remarks on hell come from his eighty-fourth homily. Maximus's distinction between gnomic and natural will is made usually in connection with his Christology, and can be found, for example, in his third and seventh *Opuscula*, English translations of which can be found in Andrew Louth's *Maximus the Confessor*, published in 1996 by Routledge. The quotation from Aquinas regarding the greater good and the lesser evil is found in *De veritate* q. 5, a. 5, ad 3; he goes on to write, *"ideo ad hoc quod aliqua bona maiora eliciantur, permittit aliquos in mala culpa*

cadere, quae maxime secundum genus sunt odibilia":
"thus, in order that certain greater goods might be
brought forth, [God] permits some to fall into evil crimes,
of a kind most odious."

Calvin's claim that God predestined the fall is found in
the *Institutes* III, 23, 7. His reasoning is fairly elementary:
since God has perfect foreknowledge of all that will happen, we must affirm that in electing to create this world
he directly determined all of its contingencies. Clearly he
thinks of God's free decision to create as an arbitrary
choice among an infinity of possible worlds, for otherwise his argument would carry no force. But this is a defective view of creation, surely, and it reflects certain
weaknesses inherent in Calvin's Christology. Not that
there is space here to argue the point, but surely we must
say that this is the world God creates because it is the
world of Jesus, and that there is nothing "arbitrary" —
there cannot be — in any act of God. That is, Jesus is not
an accidental identity assumed by the divine Logos:
when God empties himself of his divine glory and becomes a man, this is the man he is; and so, fallen or un-
fallen, this is God's true world. My argument assumes a
"supralapsarian" theology of the Incarnation, of course,
which is the overwhelming consensus of Orthodox tradition, and which is undoubtedly — despite the doubt of
even so great a theologian as Aquinas on this score —

correct (but all of this is an argument for another time). Calvin's rejection of any distinction between divine will and divine permission appears in *Institutes* III, 23, 8.